"When a Girl's Beautiful"
The Life and Career of Joi Lansing

RICHARD KOPER

"When a Girl's Beautiful" — The Life and Career of Joi Lansing
© 2019 Richard Koper. All Rights Reserved.

No part of this book may be reproduced in any form or by any means, electronic, mechanical, digital, photocopying or recording, except for the inclusion in a review, without permission in writing from the publisher.

Published in the USA by:
BearManor Media
PO Box 71426
Albany, Georgia 31708
www.bearmanormedia.com

Hardcover: ISBN 978-1-62933-464-6
Paperback: ISBN 978-1-62933-463-9

Printed in the United States of America.
Book design by Brian Pearce | Red Jacket Press.

Table of Contents

Foreword.. 7
Acknowledgements.. 9
Preface.. 13
Introduction... 21

Chapter 1: The Thirties
Early Youth.. 31

Chapter 2: The Forties
Teenage Model and Movie Starlet...................... 37
High Hopes.. 47

Chapter 3: The Fifties
Hard Times.. 67
The Monroe Comparison................................ 73
Love That Joi!... 89
Sinatra's Girl.. 103
Blonde Ambition... 115

Chapter 4: The Sixties
New Directions... 133
The Singer, Not the Song............................... 145
Marriage on the Rocks.................................. 163
Career Opportunities.................................... 181

Chapter 5: The Seventies
Private Times... 191
The End... 207

Filmography.. 211
Television Appearances................................. 251
Pin-Ups... 289
Magazine Cover Gallery................................ 299
Bibliography.. 327
Index.. 329
About the Author.. 333

For Alexis

Keep young and beautiful,
It's your duty to be beautiful.
Keep young and beautiful,
If you want to be loved.

ANNIE LENNOX

Foreword

There are very few people in this world who are so dedicated to much of anything, especially searching for connections to a long deceased 50's and 60's blonde bombshell. Richard Koper is one of those very special individuals.

He has spent hundreds of hours researching the life and career of beautiful actress and singer Joi Lansing. His search has revealed acquaintances and intimate friends of Joi, whom he has interviewed in this book.

He has written countless letters, emails and Googled the internet until he located people who knew and worked with her. Richard's investigation into Joi's life and career is nothing short of intrepid.

Richard has shown respect for the memory of Joi, which is the reason why I am endorsing his book. Joi was the greatest love of my life and Richard has treated her with dignity. My goal is to keep her memory alive, and with Richard's help, she will not be forgotten.

ALEXIS HUNTER
"Joi Lansing — A Body to Die For. A Love Story."

Acknowledgements

This book is dedicated to my dear friend Alexis Hunter. "You were the light in Joi's last dark years. Thank you so much for sharing your story of love, friendship and dedication and for keeping Joi's memory alive."

Many thanks to Joi's relatives John Shupe and Beverly Watkins. John, thank you for being so helpful answering my questions and providing me with photos from the family archives. Thank you for trusting me, writing Joi's story. Beverly, thank you very much for your help and for the photos you provided.

I'm very grateful for the help of the following people: Preston Reese, who did his own research on Joi and provided me with his notes. The late Gloria Pall, a lovely lady who shared many stories with me about her days in Hollywood. Bill Corcoran, Joi's press agent, thank you for sharing your memories with me. Elaine Hollingsworth aka Sara Shane, thank you very much for talking to me about your time at MGM. Wesley L. Fox, thank you for responding to my letter to tell me more about your date with Joi. Lisa Davis, although her memories of Joi are less positive than most of the people I interviewed, she took the time to talk with me and was gracious and very friendly. Will 'Sugarfoot' Hutchins, a positive and delightful man, thank you for answering my letter. Mike Marx, thank you for sharing your story with me and letting me use your unique photographs. Chris Mitchum, a very friendly man, thank you for sharing your memories about working with Joi. Trini Lopez, a delightful man, thank you for granting me an interview to talk about your friendship with Joi. Bill Hayes and Ron De Salvo, two marvelous men who worked with Joi in Las Vegas. Thank you both for being so helpful in recollecting your memories. Barrie Chase-Kaufman; a very nice lady with whom I had a pleasant conversation about Joi and the other Hollywood blondes she worked with.

I also like to thank the following people for sharing their stories with me and letting me share their unique photos: Cliff Laureno, Craig Marin, Ronald E. Giles, Susan Moody Carpenito, Terry Moore, Michel

De Carvalho aka Michel Ray, Dwayne Hickman, Keith Thibodeaux aka Richard Keith, Karen Sharpe, Laurie Mitchell, Eddie Hodges, Brett Halsey, Roberta Linn, Dyanne Thorne, Leslie Todd, Pete Edgar, Barbara Luna, Mamie Van Doren, Max Baer Jr., Francine York, Christopher Riordan, Sandra Piller, Clarence Potter, Edward 'Torchy' Smith, Gary Lorig, Bill Marx, Lauren Angelich, Nancy 'Czar' Bretzfield, June Wilkinson, Bill Dolive and finally I like to thank author Joseph Dougherty for permitting me to quote from his book *Comfort and Joi*.

Preface
The Mormon Movie Star

During her career, the press loved to mention that Joi Lansing was a Mormon and a teetotaler. It contrasted wonderfully with her sexy pin-up image. Although the harmless information seemed correct, the truth was different.

As early as 1950, the press started mentioning that Joi was a non-drinker and non-smoker: "Incidentally, this vivid girl, who says she doesn't go to church every Sunday, neither drinks nor smokes and her extreme passion for cleanliness extends to mental and moral as well as physical surroundings."[1] An article in *The Ogden Standard-Examiner*, mentioned that she had just lost a cigarette commercial job because, not being a smoker, she could not inhale convincingly.[2]

In 1956, the 'religious sex-bomb' tag surfaced. *Tempo* magazine featured her in a cover story. The article read in part, "You would think that posing for glamor pictures comes easily to Joi Lansing. After all, she does it so well. But just the opposite is true. As a devout Mormon, who does not drink, smoke or go nightclubbing, Joi can't help feeling troubled at being called onto display her charms for still photographers."[3]

The 'devout Mormon' characterization was replicated in another magazine about a year later. This article added, "The whistle-bait blonde was born in Utah. She keeps in shape by eating well, then working it off at a gym."[4]

Second cousin Beverly Watkins relates Joi's virtues to her Christian background. "I am sure that the values Joi had were from her bringing up in the gospel of Jesus Christ. The church is very proud of celebrities of which there are many who are members in the music and theater."[5]

1 *The Salt Lake Tribune*, February 11, 1950.

2 January 15, 1956.

3 July 10, 1956.

4 *People Today*, June 1957.

5 Source: email contact with author.

In contrast, Joi's cousin John Shupe's opinion is that not drinking nor smoking had nothing to do with any religious affiliation. "Those involved with her career promotion thought it was good publicity to let people say she didn't drink or smoke due to her Latter Day Saints religion, as it was unique and not harmful information even if it was inaccurate about her church affiliation. She did have a strong interest in her own good health. As I remember she was enthusiastic about a healthy nutritious drink she would prepare for herself in an electric blender. If I remember correctly, she called it tiger milk."[6]

Joi would also discuss her secrets of staying young and healthy with her press agent Bill Corcoran. "During a lunch at the famous Garden of Allah on Sunset Boulevard in 1958, Joi told me her secret to keeping her figure was drinking a health food drink called 'Tiger's Milk' and swimming in the nude in the pool at her Hollywood Hills home. I took the information and planted an item in New York columnist Earl Wilson's column."[7]

Members of the Church of Jesus Christ of Latter Day Saints are baptized when they are old enough to be accountable for their actions, which is about the age of eight. From that moment, the members are accountable for any mistakes they make in the future and have to take the sacrament on a weekly basis to renew their covenants made at their baptism. Because Joi moved away from Utah when she was six years old, she wasn't baptized, making her no member of the Church. Furthermore, Joi's mother no longer practiced her Mormon beliefs.

John Shupe mentions that he and his family were non-active members of the LDS church. He doesn't recall Joi being active or a member of any religion. "I have no knowledge of her being a member of the Mormon church. I do know when she was in Ogden she loved going to my grandfather's LDS ward close to his home. I recall her saying how much she enjoyed singing with everyone, and that was the main reason she would attend Sunday services. I never went to that church with her, as I was told by the ward leadership that I was not welcome due to the fact that I lived in another ward (church district). When I once attempted to go to that ward, as I remember it was called the Mount Ogden Ward at 27th Street at Tyler Avenue in Ogden, I was turned away. Joi was welcome because she was from out of town."[8]

Joi's close friend and companion Alexis Hunter recalls, "Actually, Joi had no religious affiliation, contrary to all the studio publicity around that issue. She was born in Salt Lake City and into a Mormon family, but her

---

6   Source: email contact with author.

7   Source: email contact with author.

8   Source: email contact with author.

mother drifted away from the LDS Church soon after she was born, and eventually gravitated to Christian Science. Though Joi didn't personally belong to any church, she was spiritual in nature. She practiced what everyone else preached and adhered to the most important tenet of religion, to treat everyone as you would like to be treated."[9]

Joi made a gimmick of the 'Mormon versus Sexpot' image her entire

Joy Lansing and Dolores Donlon, MGM 1948.

career. In 1970, she was quoted about how her religious upbringing conflicted with her career. "I'm a Mormon, you know, I was brought up very strictly. The entire exposure I've had, ever since I first signed with MGM when I was fourteen years old, has been somewhat traumatic for me." She held on to the figment that she wasn't using alcohol nor that she smoked. "I don't smoke, and I don't drink. Don't print that…or my entire image will be ruined. I used to resent it terribly when I was called a sexpot, but eventually I overcame this feeling. And soon I had a good many motion picture, TV and night club parts."[10]

9 Hunter, Alexis. *Joi Lansing — A Body to Die For. A Love Story.* Albany: Bear Manor Media, 2015.

10 *Men's Digest,* July 1970.

While researching Joi's life and career, I didn't hear a bad story or negative memory about her. She's described as "down-to-earth, modest, friendly, warm and caring." Through talking with people who knew Joi intimately, worked with her or met her on diverse occasions, I was able to paint a picture of a classy lady who tried very hard to become a star, settled for being 'a face and figure,' and through her professionalism gained the respect of almost all the people who encountered her. Leslie Todd remembered her stepmother as "a fabulous person, very sweet, kind, generous and totally unpretentious. She would never say anything unkind or mean about anyone. Everyone adored her."[11]

Child actor Eddie Hodges worked with Joi in *A Hole in the Head* (1959). "I just met her once when she came to visit Mr. Sinatra on the set. She was very beautiful and down-to-earth. Lots of charisma."[12]

Movie and TV starlet Gloria Pall encountered Joi several times. "I knew Joi Lansing very well. She was just lovely. She had the most beautiful complexion and gentle speaking voice. In *Hot Shots*, I worked with Joi. I wore a gold sequin dress which the Bowery Boys reacted to, as I walked across the room. That was a real walk on! I also worked with Joi in *Son of Sinbad*. We were both dressed in harem costumes and veils. The next time was in 1955 on *The Bob Cummings Show*. I had a good part in one of the episodes. She was in rehearsal and came over to greet me."[13]

Actress Mamie Van Doren encountered Joi numerous times on photo shoots and other occasions the studios sent their starlets to. "Joi was a sweetheart. I didn't know her personally, but I always admired her spirit. She came on the scene before me. I remember seeing her on the *Love That Bob* TV series."[14] Actor Will Hutchins, remembered working with Joi very well. "My memory of working with Joi is filtered with only good feelings. I wish she'd been under contract to Warner Bros., but I'm sure she did just fine outside the wall. Thinking about her, I'd easily rate Joi Lansing as one of my top ten favorite leading ladies on *Sugarfoot*. She had beauty and a light touch of comedy as well."[15]

Actor and dancer Christopher Riordan grew up watching Joi Lansing on TV. "Like most people, I considered her a part of that group of

---

11 Source: email contact with author.

12 Source: email contact with author.

13 Source: email contact with author.

14 Source: email contact with author.

15 Source: mail contact with author.

blonde actresses that were trying to cash in on the Marilyn Monroe craze. Truthfully, I didn't give her much credit one way or the other, until I finally arrived in Hollywood, and began running into her at various functions. Mainly, the Horoscope parties that Carroll Righter used to give. Joi was often there, and it was then that I discovered she was a lovely young lady. I never dreamed that I would ever work with her;

Hot Cars, 1956.

but in a sense, that did happen. In the end, I would say I liked Joi, and I respected how she handled herself. I don't know anyone who had anything bad to say about her. Personally, I think she was dealt a poor hand. She was lovely, smart and talented. But she was limited. Her career never really took off, her marriages all ended unhappily, and she died way too young."[16]

Actress Francine York had befriended Joi in the 1960s. "She was an absolutely marvelous girl and she was very much into health and nutrition. I remember that she got me started on the tiger milk and bars which was like the first health food that ever came out. She looked like the sexy bombshell, but she was a very much down-to-earth girl and just a lovely

---

16 Source: email contact with author.

human being and I felt very saddened when she died of cancer of the breast. I think she had her breasts enlarged or something. I was very much shaken by her death because she was a lovely human being."[17]

In the later part of her career, Joi appeared on the popular television series *The Mothers-In-Law*, starring Kaye Ballard and Eve Arden. One of Kaye's funniest on-set memories involves her voluptuous guest star. "Joi had huge breasts. In one scene, I was sitting in front of her and looking up, and honestly couldn't see her face. We just couldn't stop laughing."[18] Joi was in on the joke and had no problem to mock herself and ridicule the image she created. At the time she was unaware of the ailment that was developing due to her physical enhancements.

My own fascination with Joi Lansing started when I saw her in a photograph with actress Barbara Nichols, a publicity still for *Who Was That Lady?* (1960). She had an immediate appeal on me. I'd experienced this once before, when I watched *Some Like it Hot* (1959) with the charismatic and beautiful Marilyn Monroe. I became curious about the story behind this alluring, blonde pin-up actress. You'll understand that it was much harder to learn more about Joi than it was getting to know Marilyn's life story. Over the years, I've found out more about her career as an actress and singer but was in the dark about her private life. When I came in contact with her cousin John Shupe, he welcomed me to learn more about the Joi he knew; a woman with a kind soul and loving heart. And when I met Alexis Hunter, I learned about the tragic last years of Joi's life. Alexis confided in me to read about her intimate relationship with Joi, before her book was officially published.

When a Girl's Beautiful — The Life and Career of Joi Lansing is a biography about a woman who was as reserved in her private life as she was as a celebrity. She was much more than how she's described in most of the articles and tidbits written about her, "The Mormon Movie Star," "Frank Sinatra's regular bed-mate," "Movie Starlet turned Café Singer," "TV's answer to Marilyn Monroe," etcetera. Ninety years after her birth, Joi Lansing still holds a special place in many people's memories and hearts. To some she may be considered a tragic person, but I hope that's not the way you will think of her when you've read her story. I hope you will remember her as the shining star and loving human being she truly was.

---

17 Source: email contact with author.

18 *The Spectrum*, November 11, 2015.

Introduction

"When a girl's beautiful, the world lays at her feet." We assume that life is easier, and opportunities are presented on a golden serving tray, for someone with striking features and an attractive physique. It's a well-known fact that pretty people are assigned with positive qualifications, just because of their looks. However, fairness is no guarantee for happiness.

In the 1950s and 1960s, Joi Lansing was a well-known Hollywood starlet. She was known for her hourglass figure and lovely face, rather than her acting skills. She started out in show business as Joy Loveland, a name she earned from her stepfather. She played bit parts, made cameo appearances and had featured roles in low-budget movies. But she is largely remembered for her tremendous output in television during its Golden Age. Mature men, teenage boys and girls gasped over her beauty while watching TV's *Superman*, *The Bob Cummings Show* and *The Beverly Hillbillies*.

Joi grew up in the years of the Great Depression, but she wasn't raised in poverty. Her grandfather provided for everything his little blonde angel desired. Still the girl wasn't spoiled, she was a sweet child with a sunny character. As a teenager, her striking good looks were noticed by talent scouts and through winning beauty contests, she was signed by MGM. She was dominated by her mother; who wanted her to reach the highest level in showbusiness.

Her father had left when she was one year old. Joi kept searching for a father figure her entire life. After three failed marriages, and with the last one still in mind, Joi commented, "My marriage made me so unhappy, I went to nightclubs every night. Now I stay home and study. I'm mostly supposed to be a dumb blonde on TV, but I really put a lot of thought into it. Besides, night-clubbing just ruined my figure."[1]

Frank Sinatra was a close friend, as were Dean Martin, Peter Lawford and Sammy Davis Jr. The so-called Rat Pack attracted beautiful women.

---

1 *TV Guide* for week July 6-12, 1957.

Joi belonged to the group of starlets that regularly were called upon to make a cameo appearance in one of their productions.

Producers and advertising agencies referred to her as "the girl who keeps the iceboxes closed," as they were more than convinced that male viewers, who otherwise might wander to the refrigerator for refreshments, kept to their seats when Joi's curvesome form undulated across their TV screens. Television critic Steven H. Scheuer wrote in November 1955, "If a TV award were given for the busiest blonde in Hollywood, Joi Lansing would get it. For the past year, she's averaged two shows a week. Whenever a blonde baby doll is needed for a scene, Joi gets the call. One look at her and you can see why. You can start from the ankles and move up, or vice versa — and you'll find that the usual adjectives fit her perfectly — trim, compact and well rounded."

Joi was very conscious about her appearance but wasn't confident about her looks. She was especially insecure about her round facial features. Beverly Watkins, her second cousin, recalled, "My grandmother and Joi's grandmother are sisters. Aunt Grace, as she was called, was a beautiful woman herself. Mostly all I can remember of Joi was that she never took a front shot because she said her cheeks were too fat. I also remember her cleaning her face with mounds of cold cream."[2]

In a 1955 interview, Joi commented, "I look so much better in color. In the movies, an actress is surrounded by a corps of beauty experts, you know, wardrobe mistress, makeup man, hair stylist. You don't have those on TV. You have to furnish your own wardrobe most of the time. You have to worry about your hair and all, and you pray everything comes off all right."

In the early 1950s, actress Karen Sharpe was starting out as an actress. She met Joi on various promotional occasions. "I think I met Joi Lansing probably on some of the *Photoplay* movie magazines things that we did for publicity reasons. I met a lot of people on those kinds of shoots. She was very nice, but we were also worried about how we looked, so it wasn't like we were best friends or anything like that. You know, this business is a hard business. You're judged every minute. How you look, how you behave. It was very much a class system that way."

Like Joi, Karen worked all the time, so there wasn't time for friendship. "When you look back on it, we were so lucky to be in this industry. We were appreciated; today it means nothing. You can be in one film, win an Academy Award and be forgotten the next day. In those days, it meant

---

2 Source: email contact with author.

something. We were real stars and were taught to behave like that. We didn't call anybody by their first name, it was a very, very formal time."³

Friend Bill Marx set the nightclub acts for her and did her musical arrangements in the 1960's. "Joi was as sweet as you would wish anyone to be, and as insecure about her professional life as anyone could be. She told me that she felt that the only reason she ever got hired was because of her beauty. And in spite of that neurotic concern, she managed to carve out a pretty successful career."⁴

Step-daughter Leslie Todd underlined Joi's willpower and forte to build a career in showbusiness. "I think that Joi really loved being an actress and she worked very hard to try to get parts. Hollywood is not for the light hearted or lazy persons. You have to be able to cope with a lot of rejection and disappointments. One of her favorite roles was playing a model in a tv show called *Love That Bob*. And everywhere we went she was always gracious about signing autographs. She never said no."⁵

While walking around New York City in the Spring of 1964, photographer and celebrity spotter Santiago Rodriguez saw her walking down the street. He experienced her willingness to pose for him. "I was an up and coming celebrity photographer in my teens in NYC and always took my camera everywhere. My haunts were Sardi's, TV tapings, and the big fancy hotels in the area, and of course Broadway shows. This particular day was a Saturday and Miss Lansing literally passed me on the street. I did a total turnaround until she passed what I found to be suitable background. She posed willingly and was quite pleasant and way better looking in person than on any TV show. I remember she may have been carrying a bag or something and set it down near where I posed her, so it would not clutter up the photo. She was not wearing sunglasses or anything and I believe she was alone. I must also tell you that she did turn heads, there is no way that someone like that, and looking the way she did that day, could possibly walk down the street and not be spotted. Mind you, they may not have known who she was, but look they surely did. My eye was trained so I would have spotted her a block away. I had another encounter with her at the TV taping of a show called *Girl Talk*, hosted by Virginia Graham."⁶

3 Source: telephone interview with author, 06-04-2016.

4 Source: email contact with author.

5 Source: email contact with author.

6 Source: email contact with author. Instead of the *Girl Talk* show, Joi appeared on *The Virginia Graham Show* with Peter Lupus and singer Charo on May 3, 1971.

Whilst newspaper columnist Dorothy Killgallen was on vacation, guest columnists were asked to write a piece for the *Voice of Broadway* section. Joi wrote hers in August 1965. "For the record, my vital statistics are 39-23-35. That, however, is not all there is to me — it had better not be if one has any thoughts of an enduring career in the fiercely competitive entertainment industry these days. Once and for all time, I'd like to lay to rest that old saw that a girl can be lastingly successful in this tough business if she comes equipped with a pretty face and big bosom, period. No, it isn't so — it never really was! Sure, you can get your picture all over the papers. There's nothing a photo editor likes better than a picture of a well-stacked female, preferably in a bathing suit. But, that's not show business. Ultimately, it's a talent that pays off, and always will. Of course, I'm delighted that Mother Nature was bountiful with me. I enjoy being a girl, and I enjoy those attributes that make a girl a girl. It's also true that my face and figure have opened many a door for me. After all, as long as men are men, a shapely female will have an advantage anywhere, whether up for a Broadway audition, or out for a job as a filling clerk in an insurance office. That is, as long as men are doing the hiring, and it so happens that virtually all the agents, producers, talent bookers, etc. in the entertainment industry are men. But once you've gotten that audition, that's about as far as the face and figure will take you. Beyond that point, it's a question of talent-to-survive. Broadway and Hollywood, and any place else where the bright lights shine, is strewn with the broken hopes of well-built girls who came seeking fame and fortune in show business with those credentials alone. They're inevitably doomed to failure and frustration.

"All one has to do is look at the record of well known, well-endowed gals who succeeded in show business. In each case, there was a considerable talent to go along with the traffic-stopping topography. The queen of them all, the late Marilyn Monroe, matured into an extraordinarily skillful actress before her tragic death. Lana Turner, the first of the great 'sweater girls' more than two decades ago, was always a superior actress. Jane Russell's another who proved she had more than a breathtaking façade. Witness her very successful career as a singer and recording star. If you saw Anita Ekberg in *La Dolce Vita* you know this celebrated 'body' can act. Kim Novak handles dramatic roles capably. Marie Wilson is an accomplished comedienne, Mamie Van Doren sings up a storm with one of the slickest nightclub acts in the business. Monique Van Vooren is a gifted light comedy actress and sophisticated song stylist who's been spotlighted in some of the nation's toniest hotels and night spots. By contrast, many bosomy ladies who flashed to rapid fame vanished gradually from the spotlight as discriminating audiences and industry judges realized there was nothing more substantive involved, that once the appraising glances were over no talent emerged to occupy the attention. I'd rather not mention names lest I be accused of the supposed feminine trait of cattiness."

Joi described how she got her start in the business. She mentioned her bit parts in several movies and her participation on *The Bob Cummings Show*. "I appreciated it, yet I grew to realize I was going nowhere. I was used solely for decoration and never given a chance to act or sing. But I always wanted to sing and knew I could. I also knew that I had a flair for light comedy. At around this time, a personal manager named Ray Evans came into my life. He saw more in me than just a body. He asked me to come East for a singing stint at the Living Room which was well-received by Manhattan night club goers and the reviewers. That engagement was a kind of vindication for me. Ray also got a fine singing teacher, new vocal arrangements, a new wardrobe, and the new Joi Lansing was born — a girl who could do more than look provocative in a low-cut dress. Nightclub engagements followed at the Americana and Waldorf Astoria in New York, the Shoreham in Washington, the Queen Elizabeth in Toronto, many other locales, and I also was given the opportunity to sing on several network television shows. Now that everything's coming up roses for me, I've been doing a little stock-taking. It's been a matter of personal pride to prove I could make it on my talents and cast aside the image solely as a 'body.' Yes, I'm still glad about those measurements; they helped. But I'm even happier that I didn't have to rely on them alone."[7]

1955 August, United Kingdom.

Besides beauty Joi possessed brains, and on some occasions, she liked to show it. Journalist Ken Mayer recalled, "Joi spoke to friends often about her open admiration for writer Norman Mailer, and at the

[7] Copyright 1965, King Features Syndicate, Inc.

time she was in Boston [in the late sixties], Mr. Mailer had residence in Provincetown. And at least once a week, he would journey to town and spend a night or two at his suite in 46 Beacon. In conversation one night, I mentioned to Joi that Norman Mailer was in town, and she asked if there was any possible way she could meet him. A friend of mine at the time owned 46 Beacon and through his offices, a dinner meeting was arranged. Mailer, as most readers know, is a complex man. He can either kill you with kindness, or just plain kill you. But Joi so captivated Mailer, that he was not only at his self-imposed best, but was gracious beyond belief. And even he was amazed at the amount of literary knowledge displayed by her and for over three hours they made literary talk while the rest of us listened. At dinner's end, it was hard to tell which of the two had been the more impressed with the other — Mailer, who had met a well-matched combination of beauty and brains — or Joi, who had found him to be delightfully provocative, yet pleasingly informative. The evening was well spent."[8]

Joi Lansing lived her life at the mercy of the entertainment industry's wishes and demands and experienced its obsession with perfect looks and eternal youth. She's one of Hollywood's tragic figures, who lost her life in the attempt to stay young and beautiful at any cost. If she was nothing else, Joi Lansing was a sincere and sensitive person, and if there was anything about her makeup to the contrary, her actions toward others certainly gave lie to its existence. Gifted by nature with a face and figure that ofttimes proved as much of a deterrent as an asset, she never quite reached the zenith of a successful career, yet many times she came within shooting distance of it. And like many beautiful symbols of her time, she made a premature exit from an unfulfilled life.

---

8 The *Boston Herald*, Aug. 15, 1972.

Joi at the Hal Roach studios, 1948.

Joi on the set of *Bat Masterson*, 1959.

Nightclub, with Glenda Farrell, 1959.

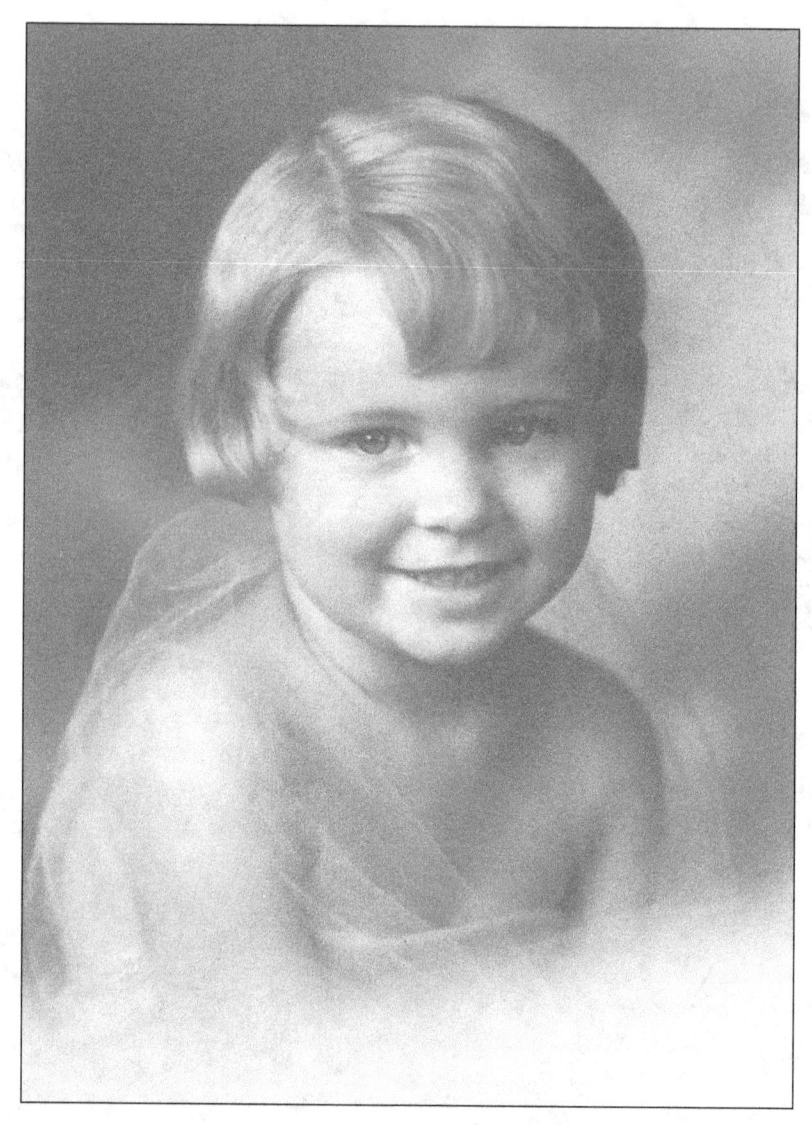

Chapter 1: The Thirties

Early Youth

Joi Lansing was the only child of Jack Glen Brown (b. June 7, 1900) and Virginia Grace Shupe-Brown (b. August 10, 1908). Jack was born in Lehi, Utah. His parents were James J. Brown (b. 1880) and Elizabeth Valeria Marshall (b. 1883). Virginia was born in Ogden City, Utah. Her parents were Annette Grace Rice (b. December 18, 1885) and Andrew Ray Shupe (b. May 28, 1885), a building contractor. Grace and Ray were married on September 17, 1906.

Virginia and her brother Raymond belonged to a prosperous family. *The Ogden Standard-Examiner* of April 3, 1926 mentioned that Virginia's parents made a real estate transfer of a part of lots in Ogden City for the amount of $4000, which was a lot of money at the time. Both Virginia and Jack's parents were Mormons and were members of the Church of Jesus Christ of Latter Day Saints. Grace and Ray Shupe were not happy when their nineteen-year-old daughter started dating Jack, a shoe salesman and part-time musician. However, the headstrong girl prevailed and Virginia and Jack were married on November 29, 1927, in Farmington in the county of Davis.

A year and a half later, a baby girl was born. The beautiful round-faced infant was christened Joy Rae Brown. She saw the light of day at 9:40 pm on April 6, 1929, at the Holy Cross Hospital in Salt Lake City. When Joy was less than a year old the family moved to Ogden. In the 1930s Ogden was Utah's second largest city with 40,272 inhabitants, behind Salt Lake City with 140,267 inhabitants. Joy was born on the brink of the Great Depression, that started in the Autumn of 1929. At the height of the Depression, in 1933, 32 percent of the population of the state of Utah was receiving all or part of their food, clothing, shelter, and other necessities from government relief funds. And in the nation as a whole, Utah's marriage rate dropped as did the birth rate. The divorce rate rose.

The totally different background of Jack and Virginia soon brought tension between the couple. Jack, being a musician, was away from home several days a week, leaving Virginia by herself with the baby. Returning from work in the wee hours, Jack was often under the influence of alcohol. When their daughter was just one year old, the couple decided to break up. Virginia and her toddler moved in with her parents. Joy was primarily raised by her grandparents. She was the apple of her grandfather's eye and he went out of his way to give his beloved granddaughter anything she desired. Joy set her mind on a drama career at the early

Joy and Virginia, 1929.

age of five, after she'd danced and acted in a Sunday School play. Every weekend, she went to the cinema with her mother and grandmother. Seeing Shirley Temple dance and sing, the little girl knew that she wanted to do just that.

Eventually Virginia found herself a new fiancé, Ogden born Vernon Loveland (b. 1906). He was working as a waiter when he met Virginia. At the time Vernon was still married to Thelma Terry. He divorced her to marry Virginia on November 5, 1933. It was his third marriage.[1] The

---

1 Vernon Chauncey Loveland (March 10, 1906) was married to Gwene Leone Cottle on May 29, 1924 and married Thelma Terry on February 27, 1931.

newlyweds rented a house in Salt Lake City and Joy adopted the name of her stepfather. The girl was to experience a happy home with her mother for the first time.

In 1935, the Lovelands decided to move to Los Angeles, California. Joy later recalled, "When mother moved to Hollywood she took me with her, of course — and I kicked and screamed all the way. I was desperately in love. His name was Ted Elliott, I think he lived on 32nd South and he was about my age, which was six. I was sure I'd never recover."[2] It's more likely that the young girl protested fiercely to her mother's plans to leave Utah because she was separated from her beloved grandparents. When Virginia became pregnant, the family decided to move. They rented a house for $35 a month, on 1432 Hauser Blvd. On December 20, 1940, Joy's half-brother Larry Vernon was born.

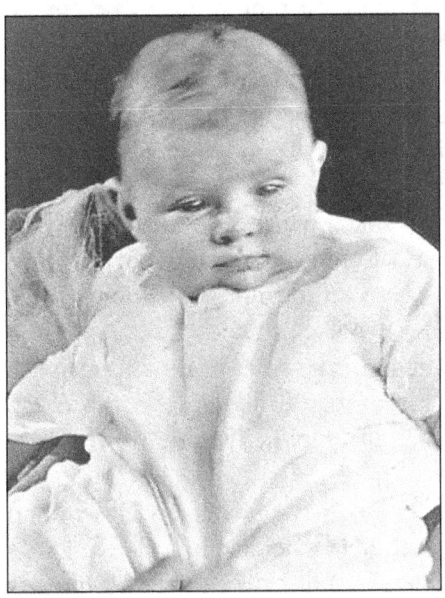

Three months old Joy Rae Brown.

During summer holidays, Joy visited Ogden to stay with her grandparents, sometimes staying as long as two months. Every Christmas, the Lovelands travelled the 724 miles back to Ogden City to visit Virginia's parents. In the Holiday season of 1941, Virginia and her parents decided that Joy would stay with her grandparents for a couple of months. On February 3 and 4, 1942, Joy appeared in a school art play at Polk Junior High School. The seventh grade presented two plays; Joy appeared as a 'Color Red' dancer in the play called *A Color's Fantasy*. Because of her grandparents, Joy had been taking dancing lessons. She was very grateful and appreciative of what her grandparents did for her. "They gave me drama lessons, piano lessons, bought me pretty clothes. They did everything for me."[3]

To her own surprise, the young girl liked the attention she got when she performed. Joy was a very quiet child. She was shy, and rather remained in

---

2 *The Salt Lake Tribune*, August 4, 1957.

3 *The Salt Lake Tribune*, February 11, 1950.

the background, keeping herself to herself. Through acting and dancing she experienced the thrill of being admired and getting noticed.

John Shupe, Joy's first cousin, remembers his grandparents as very nice people. "They were kind and caring to us grandchildren and had a close relationship with my dad. Grandpa Ray and my dad worked together as partners in home construction and were well liked by most everyone they did business with. They had a reputation of being fair, trustworthy and reliable. Joy always called grandpa Ray 'Grampy.' He was so proud of her and loved her very much. He always carried pictures of her in his wallet and was always showing the photos to most anyone he met. When my grandfather died he left a good sum of money to all family members. My grandmother, Grace, was a homemaker who had an interest in landscape drawings made with pastel chalks. Her art was very emotional, moody, with lots of scenes depicting storm clouds and threatening weather. Neither of my grandmothers drove a car. I remember Grandma Grace as being a nervous passenger. She hated high mountain passes, with roads hugging the sides of mountains with steep drop-offs. There was one mountain road called the North Ogden Divide that she refused to travel in an automobile. She said if that trip was necessary, she'd walk!"[4]

Joy was very close to her maternal grandparents and her uncle Raymond and his family. She had no contact with her father nor his relatives. Joy's close friend Alexis Hunter recalls that she didn't discuss him. "She only spoke of her grandfather, Ray Shupe. She loved him very much. He was like a father to her."[5] John adds to that, "Joy's grandfather was her father figure. I don't think she had much contact with any of the men in her mother's life."[6] Joy's one-time press agent Bill Corcoran recalled that, "Her grandfather gave her money to try her luck in Hollywood. He thought she had what it takes to make it big in Hollywood. It turned out that grandpa was right."[7]

---

[4] Source: email contact with author.

[5] Source: email contact with author.

[6] Source: email contact with author.

[7] Source: email contact with author.

Joy and Virginia, circa 1940. COURTESY OF JOHN SHUPE

Chapter 2: The Forties

Teenage Model and Movie Starlet

Joy physically developed early in her teens, and at the tender age of thirteen she started working as a teenage fashion model. She recalled that, "Strangers used to stop me and mother and tell her I should be in pictures. It got so I believed it."[1] Virginia, who was very aware of her own beauty, stimulated her daughter's first steps to stardom. *The Ogden Standard-Examiner* reported on November 25, 1942 that Joy Loveland and fellow model Alberta Gold modelled swimming suits at a Los Angeles' pool. A photograph of the event was included. The following years other modelling assignments followed and on April 1946, a teenage Joy was the cover girl of *Expose Detective Cases* magazine. She would become a regular model for other pulp fiction publications, whether as a cover girl or to illustrate the sensational stories inside these magazines. After seeing Joy's photo in magazines and the papers, former actress Rita La Roy chose her to become one of her models. She operated the Rita La Roy Junior Modeling School and Agency in Los Angeles. In the 1940s and 1950s, the agency was one of the three top modeling agencies in town.[2]

Virginia had wanted to get more out of life than being a spouse and raising children. She quarreled with Vernon about how dull her life was. When her daughter grew more beautiful by the day, Virginia never let Joy forget she was boss. Joy's relationship with her mother was troubled. She was always trying to please her, but whatever she did, it never seemed good enough. John Shupe remembers his aunt as a beautiful woman who was conscious of fashion and her appearance in public. "She was emotional and believed in fortune tellers and such. I always questioned her sincerity toward family members."[3]

Alexis knew Joy's mother as a self-centered woman and remembered that Virginia always wanted to better herself and didn't attach herself to

---

1 *TV Guide* for week July 6-12, 1957.

2 Other famous models the agency would represent, and who also turned to acting later on, were Merry Anders and Tippi Hedren.

3 Source: email contact with author.

her family or husband, rather to his money. Joy's sincerity toward family members is not questioned by Alexis and John, who emphasized that, "Her love for family was consistently pure, sincere and heart-felt."[4] When John describes his Aunt Virginia, he mentions that, "She had a lot of continual drama going on in her life. However, she treated me well over the years. My mother for some unknown specific reason didn't speak well of Virginia. She thought Virginia was insincere when expressing her fondness to my mother, my dad and me." John continues, "I recall a snapshot of our family. It includes Larry, Joy, Virginia, Grandpa Ray, my mother and me. The photo was shot by my father and the setting was in a California parking lot. At the time, my mother insisted I sit on her lap. That really upset me because I wanted stand next to Larry. But that was not to be. Mom was insistent! I didn't figure out why, until I was in my sixties and once again looking at that old photo when I realized she had placed me on her lap and in front of her face to not be included in a photograph with Virginia."[5]

When Joy worked on her career, she simultaneously attended Dorsey High School at 3537 Farmdale Avenue in Los Angeles. Dorsey High had become a three-year school by the time of her arrival. Fellow Dorsey student Leland Welsh recalled that the 1946 annual showed a group picture of all the underclassmen, in which Joy appears as an 11th grader. In high school, she joined the theatre arts group called the Dorsey Community Players, in her senior year. She won the lead in a play, but only her drama coach seemed impressed with her dramatic ability. Everyone else raved about how beautiful she looked on stage. Leland Welsh remembered that, "She was a striking looking young lady, and played to that. She was not a shrinking violet. She dressed in a way that showed she was aware how voluptuous she was — not anything too much, just that she knew."[6] When he was eighteen-year-old, Dorsey student Don Paulsen took her out on a date. He remembered they went to Ken Murray's Blackouts on Vine Street in Hollywood in his 1934 Plymouth coupe. "I remember her beauty and how everyone looked at Joy at the theatre."[7]

Against Virginia's wishes Joy started dating Jack Shelton, an aspiring actor. A couple of months after her seventeenth birthday, Joy married after a short engagement. A year earlier Jack had returned from the war injured and after an unsuccessful back surgery, he was left partly paralyzed. Susan

4 Source: email contact with author.

5 Source: email contact with author.

6 Source: interview by Preston Reese, July 1998.

7 www.findagrave.com

Moody Carpenito was a young girl when she met Jack at the beaches of Hawaii in the 1970s. "I was a kid when I met Jack. This is many years after the fact, but I just remember the stories and all her pictures he showed of them. He often spoke of Joy lovingly."[8]

Because of her modelling and movie work, Joy had missed classes and eventually dropped out of high school. Dorsey High student Janet Coleman, who later became a Dorsey teacher, mentions, "I got out the yearbooks and went through them. Neither Joy Loveland nor Larry Loveland are listed as graduating in the Dorsey High yearbooks for 1946, 1947 or later years."[9] It was a hectic time. Joy couldn't combine going to classes during the day and attending modeling assignments in the afternoons and on the weekend.

Joy and her Grampy, 1947.
COURTESY OF JOHN SHUPE

Concentrating on her career, Joy was over the moon when she became Queen of the Hollywood Jaycees in April 1947. She was chosen to represent Hollywood in the Burbank Parade Queen contest. As a result, she was given an audition by Warner Brothers Film Studios and filled an engagement at Charley Foy's supper club in Sherman Oaks, California. Things even got better within the month, when the Hollywood Junior Chamber of Commerce chose her as the most beautiful contestant in the "Burbank on Parade." Joy landed the title of "Miss Hollywood." She received movie tests beside several wardrobe gifts. Joy's movie test at Columbia resulted in her movie debut, in the aptly named *When a Girl's Beautiful* (1947).

The very thin story of this B-movie comedy involves model Adele Jergens, who breaks up with her agency's wealthy perfume client. When the client requests a new model for their campaign, Marc Platt, an advertising

---

8 Source: email contact with author.

9 Source: interview by Preston Reese, September 2012.

man, puts together a picture of a woman from a composite of several photos. His boss sees it, thinks that it is an actual woman, and orders him to find her. Filmed in June, the movie was shot in just twenty days. It was promoted with the tagline, "They've got talent…and show it…in the right places!" Joy was billed as one of the eight Temptation Girls. Although her part was relatively small, she appeared in several scenes and was used prominently in the publicity material for the film. On the one-sheet film poster Joy is featured twice. There's one large headshot of her next to the film's title and she is pictured sitting on the lap of Marc Platt. With her eighteen years, she was the youngest of the cast. Adele Jergens, the star of the movie, took the young girl under her wing. One year later, Adele would work with another newcomer to the business: Marilyn Monroe.

Directly after her movie debut, Joy and several other starlet models that were featured in *When a Girl's Beautiful* were used again in a comedy called *Linda Be Good* (1947). Elyse Knox and Marie Wilson starred in this B-movie about a writer who joins a Burlesque troupe to get the inside information she needs for a book she's writing. Late in July 1947, Joy filmed several Burlesque House scenes at the Wilshire Ebell Theatre in Los Angeles. The theater was also known as "The Carnegie Hall of the West." Gossip queen Louella Parsons wrote, "Its staid old cultural walls were being profaned by a shocking spectacle — a burlesque show, featuring 10 lightly clad cuties treading a specially built runway, for a movie called *Linda, Be Good*."

There are at least two accounts of how Joy was discovered by a talent scout of MGM Studios. One describes how she visited a party given in honour of showman Earl Carroll's birthday, on September 16. At the party, she met enterprising agent Ben Medford, who introduced her to MGM. Producer Arthur Freed liked the young starlet and signed her to a seven-year contract. The other story was recounted by Joy in an interview with columnist Dorothy Manners. "I was attending a Los Angeles stage show, and during the intermission this suspicious looking character came up to me in the lobby of the theatre. He said he was a talent scout for the movies — and how about it? I was so enraged I slapped him as hard as I could smack. That almost ended my career then and there because he was actually on the level and had been attending the show that day to look over the leading lady. He forgave me and called my mother about taking me to MGM for a screen test. He had obtained my telephone number from my girlfriend who had been with me at the theatre."[10]

10 *LA Examiner,* February 26, 1956.

Dorothy Manners reported in her article that after several interviews and a screen test, she was placed under contract at MGM. In that same article Joy described how she became Joy Lansing. "It was my idea to change my name from my real one, Joy Loveland, to Joy Lansing because it sounds more like an actress, don't you think?" Maybe she foresaw that, in combination with her looks, the professional name Loveland wouldn't have her recognized as a serious actress, but immediately put her in the category of "the glamour doll." The name switch didn't help to change that matter in the end.

At Metro Goldwyn Mayer with other starlets, 1946.

Joy Loveland, Columbia Pictures, 1947.

Linda Be Good, 1947.

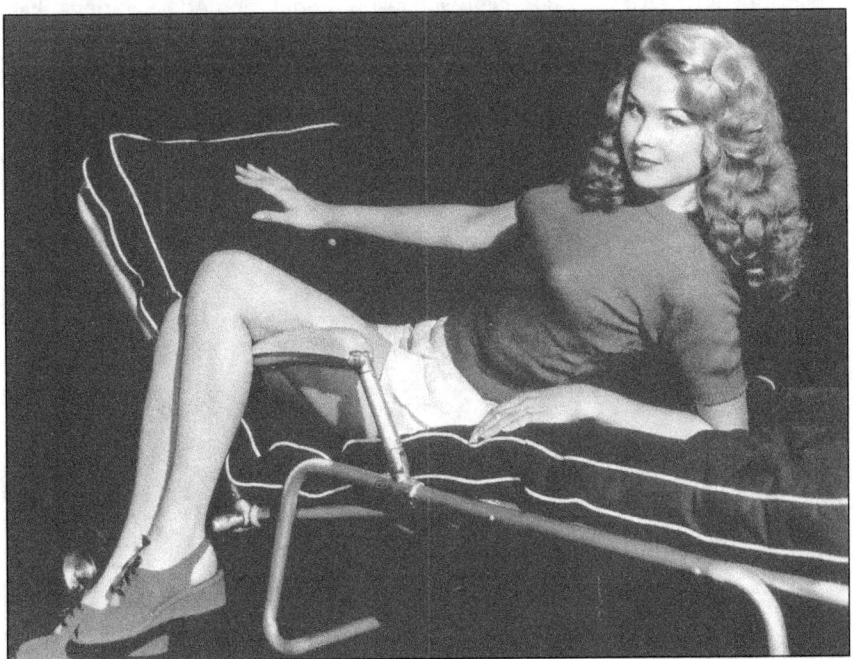

Modelling, 1947.

On the set of *When a Girl's Beautiful,* with fellow models and Adele Jergens, 1947.

Jill Lansing, Pat Alphin and Dorothy Huff in a musical short for Universal, 1947.

Title card for *Linda Be Good*, 1947.

Lobby card for *When a Girl's Beautiful*, 1947.

Warner Bros. publicity still, 1949.

High Hopes

When Metro Goldwyn Mayer took Joy in, they carefully groomed the young girl; letting her pose at the stills department for hours in several states of dress and undress, and giving her singing, dancing, diction and drama lessons. She also completed her education and received her high school diploma at the Metro Goldwyn Mayer Studio school. MGM saw her as a junior Lana Turner. Their beauty department had been critical of her boyish bottom, so in photo shoots she was to wear special panties from Frederick's with rounded padding to fill out the look the studio wanted. They also padded her bust, to make her look more voluptuous. Joy was acute enough to know why she was given a contract. "...not because of my ability," she recalled later, "just because of my appearance. The man took one look at me and offered me a contract. They didn't even give me a screen test."

Director and producer Mervyn LeRoy took a liking to Joy and acted as a mentor when Freed signed her to a contract. He had been responsible for a diverse variety of films as a director and producer. In 1938, he was chosen as head of production at MGM, where he was responsible for the decision to make *The Wizard of Oz*. He was said to have discovered Clark Gable, Loretta Young and Lana Turner. Through the years, he and Joy stayed on friendly terms.

In the winter of 1947, Joy went to a party at Dave Chasen's restaurant at Beverly Boulevard. There she met Mr. and Mrs. Hal Roach. Roach, a Hollywood producer, discussed with Joy why he had turned from movie producer to producing TV shows. He told her that television was the place to be noticed by Hollywood agents and talent scouts. In interviews he predicted, "...live studio shows around the country will act as talent scouts, with the best of the discoveries coming to Hollywood for filming."[11] Joy listened politely but didn't show much interest. TV wasn't the medium she was interested in.

MGM allowed their new contract player to take part in an independent shoestring production. She shared a scene with veteran actor Herbert Rawlinson and had two speaking lines. It's remarkable that she got

11 *Variety*, December 1948.

billing for such a small part. An equally large part, with an actress who played a stewardess, is left unmentioned in the credits. In this movie, *The Counterfeiters*, she was billed as Joyce Lansing. It was released in June 1948. On loan-out to Universal, she'd used the stage name Jill Lansing.

To refine her acting, MGM sponsored her training at the Bliss-Hayden School of Acting.[12] It was there that Joy could practice her newly learned skills. The theater was known as a showcase for young movie hopefuls, to catch the attention of important agents or studio talent scouts. In March 1948, Joy appeared in *Made in Heaven*, her first stage play. Fellow student Elaine Hollingsworth, who later became famous as Sara Shane, remembered, "We had a lovely, sweet and supportive voice coach, Mrs. Fogler. Everyone loved her. The acting coach, Lillian Burns, however, was a cruel and vindictive woman who appeared to get pleasure from making the lives of the young pretty girls miserable. She was a failed actress, and we figured we were her revenge."[13] Actress Esther Williams recalled in her autobiography, "Lillian Burns was the drama coach, and she clearly made her mark on the leading ladies of MGM. Burns was a proponent of the one-size-fits-all school of acting. She was oblivious to the fact that one might be taller, fatter, thinner, older, younger than she was. When she left a room, she left in a huff. Up went the shoulders, up went her chin. Then she snapped her head back and sailed out the door. We all learned the same mannered technique. Ava Gardner snapped her neck; so did Lana Turner and Janet Leigh. It's a wonder we all didn't end up at the chiropractor's."[14]

Another student at Bliss-Hayden was B-movie starlet Tandra Quinn. She befriended Joy and recalled, "She also attended Harry Hayden's school and theater. She got lots of work because there was always a call for the blonde, buxom beauties, and she truly was one. She was a true walking 'Lorelei' from *Gentlemen Prefer Blondes*. She was married to, or at least hung around a great deal with a good friend of my husband [Herbert Smithson] named Jack Shelton. He was good looking and a dapper dresser. He told us, 'That girl could wheedle your last dollar out of you with her wiles.' Of course, that didn't last…"[15]

---

12 The respected Bliss-Hayden School of Acting run by a husband and wife team of motion picture actress/actor Lela Bliss and Harry Hayden. In 1954, the Bliss-Hayden Theatre was acquired by Douglas Frank Bank and Jay Manford, and renamed The Beverly Hills Playhouse.

13 Source: email contact with author.

14 Williams, Esther and Diehl, Digby. *The Million Dollar Mermaid*. Orlando: Harcourt, Inc., 2000.

15 *FilmFax* #141, Summer 2015. Tandra Quinn — The Sensational Spider Woman — Spinning her Tales from the Hollywood Web! Article and interview by Alan Doshna.

Encouraged by her mother, Joy decided to leave Jack and filed for a divorce in 1948. John Shupe only once heard Joy speak about this marriage. "She said one of her biggest regrets was having divorced her first husband. She said that he was really a wonderful person and she was too young to realize what a wonderful person he was. Back in the 1950s, I was raised not to ask questions about such subjects as failed marriages or anything like that. So, I never asked many more details when she said that to me."[16] Beverly Watkins, Joy's second cousin, remembered, "Her first husband was the love of her life. She stated that was the biggest mistake she made by divorcing him. She always envied us with our children and told us we were in the best place we could be."[17]

With a movie contract at MGM, Joy really felt her acting career was moving in the right direction. She was featured in several scenes of the Fred Astaire/Judy Garland musical *Easter Parade* (1948). Joy is the first model to whom Richard Beavers sings the song "The Girl on the Magazine Cover." In that number, she was seen on the cover of *The Redbook Magazine*. In the scene where Fred Astaire sings "Happy Easter," Joy's the last shop girl to model a hat for him and she sings the lines, "This in white is exactly right. Happy Easter to you". It's the hat Joy is wearing that Astaire takes home. Joy hands him the box and therefore stands out from the other models who are standing in the back.

Elaine Hollingsworth, then known as Elaine Sterling, was also in the movie. "I remember Joy as a pretty girl with a lovely complexion. I was barely 19, and unusually innocent and pretty silly. Being there, surrounded by some of the most famous people in the world, such as the very young Liz Taylor and the divinely beautiful Hedy Lamarr, was amazing."[18] That must have been the exact feeling that Joy experienced, when she walked around the studio lot and lunched at the studio canteen. The studio announced that she was to appear in *Words and Music* (1948), and that she was to play the second lead in a biopic about entertainer and singer Helen Morgan. However, Joy didn't appear in the first movie and the production of the latter was postponed and ultimately saw the light of day, without Joy, in 1957.

When Joy studied at the Bliss-Hayden School of Acting, Marilyn Monroe was also a student there. It's most likely that the young starlets crossed paths in hallways or classrooms at the school. In the Summer of

16 Source: email contact with author.

17 Source: email contact with author.

18 Source: email contact with author.

1948, the good-looking blondes got to work together when they rehearsed for a play called *Stage Door*. Joy held the part Ginger Rogers had played on the screen. *Stage Door* opened on August 15. Louella Parsons mentioned the play in her newspaper column. She was invited by her goddaughter, Barbara Bebe Lyon, who played the movie actress in the Edna Ferber-George Kaufman play. Parsons didn't mention the acting abilities of Joy nor Marilyn in her column.

Part of her build-up was to go on dates with the male stars of the studio. When Mickey Rooney took a liking to her, Joy was over the moon. Newspaper write-ups mentioned that Mickey saw her almost every night. He took Joy to Ciro's nightclub and Dell's restaurant. Hollywood columnist Dorothy Manners reported, "Mickey Rooney, who made a point of staging it until his wife filed her divorce suit, is now stepping around with Joy Lansing. A joy to look at, I might add."[19] But it wasn't just the men at the studio that took notice of the beautiful starlet. Actress Judy Garland was attracted to Joy's wholesomeness as well and befriended Joy. Judy would follow Joy's career over the years. Alexis recalls Joy telling her that Judy's attention made her a little nervous. "When I asked why, she said that many years before, when she and Marilyn Monroe were both under contract to Metro [November/December 1949], Marilyn had invited her to go with her to Palm Springs for a little 'personal' time. Joy hardly knew Marilyn and felt uneasy going out of town with her, so she declined. Recalling that incident, Joy was somewhat apprehensive the first few times Judy came to see her show [in the 1960's], but Judy never made a pass at her and just seemed to enjoy the performance."[20] It was common at MGM and other big studios to encourage same-sex activities. Joy explained to Alexis that the studio spent tremendous amounts of money on their stars and didn't want any pregnancies.

In July, Joy and eleven other girls were chosen to portray a group of models called the Randolph Girls, to appear in Warner Bros. $2.5 million movie, *The Girl from Jones Beach* (1949). A total of 217 girls had been tested and interviewed. The movie's leading stars were Ronald Reagan and Virginia Mayo, to whom Joy was often compared. Starlet Betty Underwood, one of the models, dated Ronald Reagan while filming. "Ronnie was surrounded by girls like Virginia Mayo, Joy Lansing and Lola Albright, and the gossip columnists had fun with that."[21] Apart

---

19 June 4, 1948.

20 Hunter, Alexis. *Joi Lansing — A Body to Die For. A Love Story*. Albany: Bear Manor Media, 2015.

21 Eliot, Marc. *Reagan — The Hollywood Years*. New York: Random House LLC, 2008.

from Virginia Mayo, Joy was the only one of the girls to be featured with a photo on the six-sheet poster.

Producer Hal Roach, whom Joy had met a year earlier, had kept her in mind when he was casting his short TV film *Sadie and Sally* (1949). He had terminated his production commitment with MGM, to confine his activities exclusively to the television field. He contacted the studio and

Song writer Irving Berlin and Robert Altman, who directed the musical numbers for *Easter Parade*, and the Easter Parade Girls.

MGM allowed Joy to be loaned out. On December 22, she reported to the Hal Roach TV studios. In the comedy, she played the dumb blonde Sadie. Lois Hall played the wiser Sally. The movie was modelled after the successful short movie series of the 1930s, in which Thelma Todd and ZaSu Pitts had appeared.[22]

When the show aired, it gained a lot of attention. *Life* magazine wrote an article about Roach and the upcoming phenomenon of television, and they decided that Joy was to be their cover girl. The photo was shot by photographer John Florea. He captured Joy's wholesome beauty in

---

22 *Sadie and Sally* was a half hour in length and was to be produced at an estimated budget of $12,000 per segment.

several different photo shoots. The photos, shot on location at Santa Rosa Mountains, were made in the first week of March. Florea presented them to the *Life* magazine editors on March 19. Virginia had accompanied her daughter to the photo shoot and was pictured in several photos with her daughter. She was very proud of what Joy had achieved in such a short time in Hollywood. *Life* magazine was the leading magazine at

LIFE photo shoot, by John Florea.

the time. To grace its cover was quite an accomplishment for the young starlet. In the *Life* article, Hal Roach describes Joy as a sort of latter-day combination of Thelma Todd and Jean Harlow. He predicted that, "[Joy's] well-rounded good looks and engagingly sexy flair for slapstick comedy roles will make her one of television's leading light-headed characters."

The Spring of 1949 was an exciting time for Joy. She was chosen to join a Hollywood troupe taking entertainment to far-flung U.S. Air Force outposts in the Azores, Tripoli, Germany, France, Italy, South Africa, Alaska, Iceland, Japan and Newfoundland. On May 6, Joy and fellow starlets and aspiring singers Wanda Smith, Claudette Thornton, Rosalie Calvert, Betty Jane Howarth, Anne Ross, the sisters Caryl and Carylyn

Sietz and actress Celeste Holm, left for Europe to entertain personnel of the Military Air Transport Service.

The Salt Lake Tribune reported in a small article, "Joy's father, well-known local composer, Glen 'Jack' Brown, probably likes to think of his sprite as a singer rather than an actress. That she is, too, having a low, throaty voice that is partial to the blues, and most especially to

At MGM, with Peter Lawford, 1948.

'Embraceable You.' That is the song that evoked the most persistent wolf calls on Joy's swing around the military circuit earlier this year."[23] The mentioning of her father in this article was quite inappropriate, because Jack had never seen his daughter since he and Virginia had separated.

Joy enjoyed her performance for the soldiers and visiting the cities of Paris and Rome made an everlasting impression on the young woman. The wonderful city sites and the famous night life of these two European capitals captivated her. "You could never operate here the way they do in Hollywood, though. Imagine getting home from an evening out at 5:30 a.m. and then showing up at the studio at six!"[24] Adding, "And Rome!

23 February 19, 1950.

24 *The Salt Lake Tribune*, July 25, 1949.

Yes, I've seen Rome, and now I think I'll die if I don't get a chance to live there eventually."[25]

In May, she returned from her five-week tour. Joy and the other girls were interviewed on their arrival at Mitchel Air Force base in New York. All of them were asked the same question: "What impressed you the most about your trip?" Joy answered, "Paris interested me most — if you can call it interesting. It was fabulous! Such beautiful clothes, such beautiful sweaters. I bought the most wonderful satin skirt, which I'm going to wear tonight. Where? At the Copa. This is my very first trip to New York. I've never been here before, and so this is one of the most impressive parts of my trip. I'm really very excited about it!"[26]

Upon her arrival in Los Angeles, she had moved into a $100-a-month bachelor apartment at Larrabee Street, West Hollywood. Busy with new modelling and singing assignments, the memory of her USO tour faded. Her vocal, dancing and drama lessons kept her focused on possible new career directions. Joy decided to take matters in her own hands. The once-powerful movie moguls were under great pressure. Television was rapidly growing in popularity, leading to decreasing numbers of cinema-goers. Furthermore, the federal antitrust action separated the production of films from their exhibition. Many contract players found their contracts terminated when the studios lost their theatres and business went to the devil. Joy became a client of the William Morris Agency. On August 29, she was seen on a night out at the Mocambo with the agency's executive vice-president, Johnny Hyde.

In the fall of 1949, Joy auditioned for a featured part in *The Asphalt Jungle* (1950). Director John Huston chose Lola Albright for the role of Angela Phinlay. Neither Lola or Joy stood a chance. MGM casting director Lucille Ryman recommended rising starlet Marilyn Monroe. Johnny Hyde was a strong advocate for his young mistress also. Always gracious, Joy was to have said later, "It was such a disappointment, but when I saw Marilyn in the picture, I knew she was meant to play Angela."

MGM didn't see much more in Joy than a pretty face and figure, and after a small part in the Clark Gable comedy *Key to the City* (1950), the studio dropped her.

25 *The Salt Lake Tribune*, February 19, 1950.

26 *Nassau Daily Review-Star*, May 27, 1949.

MGM publicity photo.

MGM publicity photo.

Joy, Sara Shane and Dolores Donlon.

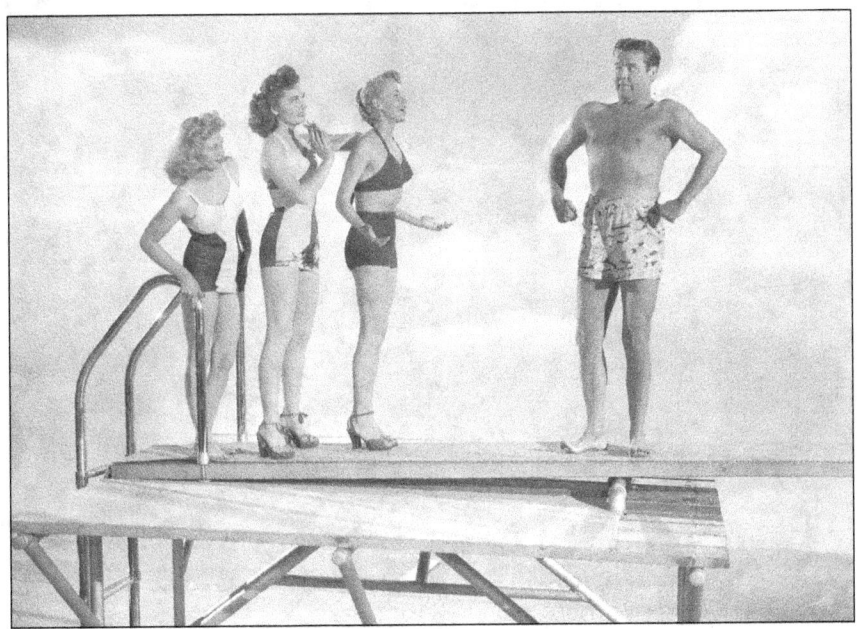

Blondie's Secret, 1949.

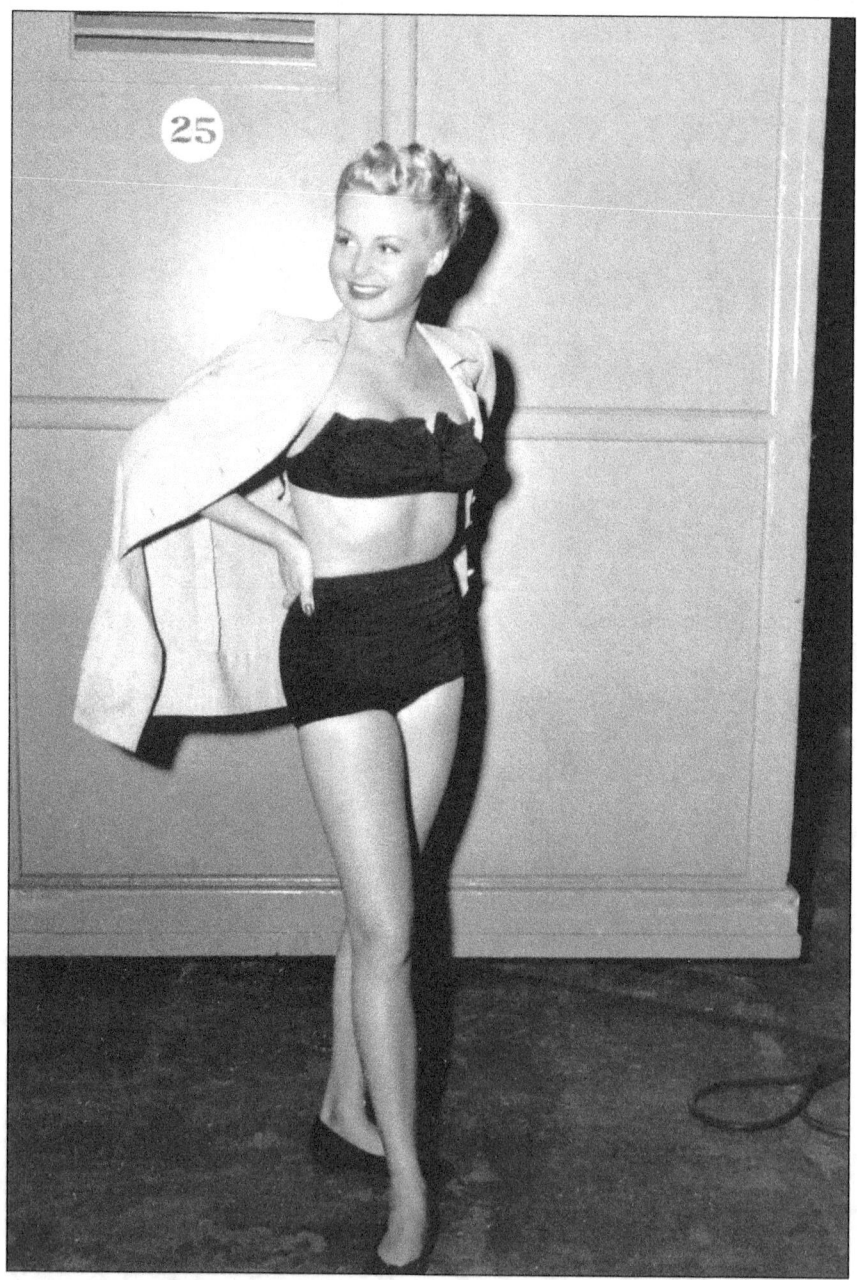

On the set of *Neptune's Daughter*, 1949.

On the beach, circa 1949.

Chapter 3: The Fifties

Hard Times

In the new year, Joy travelled to New York with her new beau and steady date Jerome Safron. They met her grandfather, and together with Joy he returned to Ogden, while Jerome stayed and attended to business. During her stay in Ogden, her uncle Raymond took her with him to several parties, to introduce his niece to the local citizenry. After a three-week visit with her grandparents, Joy returned to Hollywood in February. Grandmother Grace visited her in Hollywood several weeks later to meet Jerome. That same month, a newspaper article mentioned, "Nothing like having a rich fiancé, Joy Lansing's betrothed, Jerry Safron, has given her a car, a black mink coat, a silver fox and a leopard skin. She couldn't get cold with all that."[1]

Maybe it was a career move when Joy married the 32-year older Columbia studios' distribution executive, on March 3, in Juarez, Mexico. With the annulment of her contract at MGM, she hoped that Jerome could help her land a contract at Columbia Pictures. For their honeymoon, the couple stayed at Green Gables, Palm Springs. To break the news to the press, Joy's mother stated that the pair had been seeing each other for about a month, that they would honeymoon a few days and then fly back to Hollywood. Virginia had encouraged Joy to marry Jerome and gave the couple her blessing. She was the typical stage mother, wanting to live vicariously through her daughter's accomplishments.

In May, the William Morris Agency contacted Joy. She was considered for a part in *All About Eve* (1950). The casting director's short list for the part of George Sander's girlfriend Miss Caswell, "a graduate of the Copacabana School of Dramatic Art," included Adele Jergens, Marilyn Maxwell, Zsa Zsa Gabor, Marilyn Monroe and Joy Lansing. After interviewing Joy, Marilyn and several other actresses, he chose Marilyn for the part. She was placed on the path of fame because of her appearance in this movie. This was the second time Joy lost a movie part to the girl who was typecast in the same category as she was. One

---

1 *Democrat and Chronicle,* February 25, 1950.

wonders what would have happened with Joy's career, if she had played the part of Miss Caswell.

Joy realized she'd made a terrible mistake by marrying Jerome. On July 13, after four months of marriage only, she filed for a divorce, charging extreme cruelty. The judge handling the case denied her plea for $325 a month temporary alimony. The couple had married on the same day that

Left: Joy with her grandparents. COURTESY OF JOHN SHUPE
Right: Joy with cousins from the Rice family. COURTESY OF BEVERLY WATKINS

Jerome got a Mexican divorce from Mrs. Nancy Cornelius Brown Safron Williams, and for that reason the Lansing-Safron marriage was held invalid in Los Angeles. Jerome told the court that Joy had run him $2,000 in debt since their marriage. He said she had bought 73 dresses that cost him $7000. One week later he found himself in more hot water. His first wife had him found in contempt of court for non-payment of child support. Jerome's ex-wife brought the name of Joy into the court action, by pointing out he had spent $22,000 in his four-month marriage on her. In August, columnist Dorothy Manners wrote that Joy and Jerome had met twice to talk over their marriage headaches. Although the couple did not make up, they cleared the air between them and separated as friends.

Before the year was out, Joy met struggling young actor Lance Fuller. Up till then, he had played bit parts and wasn't too serious about his acting career. "I became more interested in films with Joy. I then began seriously to work as an actor. I met a lot of people with Joy." On Sunday February 10, 1951, Joy and Lance married in Las Vegas. They honeymooned in Utah and Nevada. Earlier they had flown to Utah to get grandfather Ray's blessing. Gloria Pall, a starlet who'd just arrived in Hollywood from New York, met the couple at a dinner party. "In 1951 when I first arrived in Hollywood, a mutual friend of Lance Fuller, a handsome actor whom Joy had just married, invited me to dinner at Joy's apartment. Both Joy's mother and Lance's mother were there. I had never heard of either one of them, but I was very impressed with Joy. She was friendly, she had a very soft kind of syrupy speaking voice and made me feel very welcome in this new Hollywood environment. I thought Joy was very beautiful, with a face like a doll. It was round, no cheek bones. Lance was very handsome and hopeful that he was star material."[2]

Joy with husband Lance Fuller, 1952.

Lance came under contract with Universal Studios and studied at their Talent School. Actor Brett Halsey was also a Universal contract player at the time and he and Lance became friends. "Lance and I were both under contract at Universal at the same time. I must have met Joy then. They were nice, I don't know anything intimate about their lives, but they were a nice couple. We weren't close, we didn't socialize, I just knew them."[3]

Lance remembered his bride being very ambitious and serious about her career. "I was on the set with her when she made *Singing' in the Rain*. I was amazed at the time by the choreography done by Gene Kelly. He was very good. Joy was in the rain sequence. She was very dedicated in becoming an actress."[4] In March, the lovebirds were separated. Lance had to enlist

---

2 Source: email contact with author.

3 Source: telephone conversation with author, 07-01-2018.

4 *ClassicImages.com*. Fuller claimed that Joy was in the rain sequence of *Singin' in the Rain*, but he was wrong about that. Joy appeared in two other scenes. Fuller was cast as a chorus boy.

in the US army. He was sent on a mission to Korea. On his return several months later, things had changed between them. When visiting Ciro's nightclub in November, Joy and Lance had a flaming battle. Joy stated, "We were terribly embarrassed. It was the first time it ever happened in public."

The early 1950s proved to be a setback in Joy's private life and movie career. She hadn't played a decent part in a movie nor attained much

Singing at the piano at her grandparents house. COURTESY OF JOHN SHUPE

work in television. In April 1951, she signed a two-picture deal with poverty row's Lippert Productions Inc. In July 1950, Joy had worked for Lippert already. She had played a very small part in *Holiday Rhythm*. Her parts in *Pier 23* and *FBI Girl* were bigger, though not substantial to the movie's plot. Nevertheless, it was Joy's image — instead of leading lady Ann Savage — that was used and featured prominently on the poster and lobby cards of *Pier 23*. In the movie, she played a cocktail waitress. She is on screen for one minute and twenty seconds, and her scene with Hugh Beaumont marks her first movie appearance with several lines of dialogue and a couple of close-ups. She was not mentioned on the title

role. In *FBI Girl*, Joy shared a scene with Jan Kayne and Audrey Totter, and was absolutely the most beautiful of the trio. *Pier 23* was released in May, and *FBI Girl* in November. Working for Lippert was a far cry from Joy's days at MGM. Actress Margia Dean also held a part in these two movies. She recalled, "These films were done fast with last minute script changes. If you hit your spot and said the dialogue, it was printed. To be pretty good in something like that is more of an achievement than being good in a big picture where you do it over and over."[5]

Joy was rumoured to appear with Gene Kelly in a featured part in *An American in Paris* (1951), but the deal fell through. The part of blonde socialite Milo Roberts was given to Nina Foch instead. Although Joy was announced by CBS Hollywood commentator George Fisher in his newspaper column of September 26 to star in *On the Riviera* (1952) in an important role, her part as a glamorous movie star was nothing more than a cameo appearance. At the time Joy was unaware that, in an indirect way, she was mentioned in a letter from Joseph I. Breen, the administrator of the Production Code Administration, to Jason S. Joy, Twentieth Century Fox's director of public relations, saying the costume for Joy showed too much breast exposure.

To earn a living, Joy took on several modelling assignments. Breast exposure certainly was no problem in this field of work. Posing for pin up artists such as Earl Moran made her some extra money. She was portrayed semi-nude, and the sitting she did for Moran marked the first time she posed sans clothes. Moran kept the painting of Joy in his personal collection of beautiful girls. She posed for several 'Detective' magazines and she landed some much-needed exposure and publicity with a page wide photo story that appeared in several nation-wide spread newspapers in September. The article featured pictures of her modelling for an ice sculpture, made by the famous ice carver Tom Sherbloom. The ice carver used Joy as his leg model for the ice statue he was carving.

She was back at the MGM studio lot to play small parts in *Singin' in the Rain*, *The Merry Widow* and *Glory Alley*.[6] *Singin' in the Rain* was made on an estimated budget of $2,540,800. Joy worked as an extra and is seen in a couple of scenes. Early in the picture she attends the premiere of Gene Kelly's *The Dancing Cavalier*, and later she's seen in the audience of the screening of Gene's movie. The movie was filmed in color, which emphasized Joy's radiant beauty. *Glory Alley*, a black and white B-movie,

---

5 *www.westernclippings.com*

6 Some articles and MGM photo snipes mention that Joy also appeared in *Lovely to Look At* (1952).

made for an estimated $971,000, showed her in a scene with fellow chorus girl Barrie Chase. "I remember Joy from that movie, and I liked her. She was very regular, very outgoing. She did showgirl things; they made more money than the dancers did. I would run into her occasionally, never on the same job. But we always talked, I always liked her. She was a very pleasant gal. Which is unusual (laughs)." Joy had no problems with her bump and grind dance moves. But Barrie had a hard time learning the moves. "In *Glory Alley*, there were four of us. I never did that kind of dancing, I was ballet-trained. We were doing a lot of bumps and grinds and I had never done that. I didn't know how to do it. And they kept telling me, 'throw your hips out more.' Lunch time came and there was a rehearsal assistant, his name was Dudley, and he said to me, 'You're not going to lunch.' He said, "I'm staying here with you and I'm going to teach you how to do this number, because if you don't have it right when they come back from lunch, you're fired.'"[7]

In Lana Turner's *The Merry Widow*, Joy's appearance got lost between twenty other girls who played dance hostesses at Maxim's. On television, she served as a regular 'Girl Friday' on the *Backstage with NTG* show in 1951 and 1952, helping the master of ceremonies Nils T. Granlund. She replaced Goldwyn girl Diana Mumby as hostess. Actress Mamie Van Doren had also appeared on the show, several years earlier. "The show was landmark — a kind of prototype of the modern talk show. It was one of the first shows originating from Hollywood. Once a week, NTG would interview a movie star, talk with the audience, and do jokes about the girls onstage who were modeling clothes or selling products."[8]

Her marriage was beginning to show cracks. Maybe Joy and Lance grew apart because they were too involved with their own careers. On the other hand, Lance's late-night drinking and gambling with his buddies didn't help to mend their relationship. On September 10, they decided to separate. Joy moved to an apartment in Burbank, twelve miles northwest of downtown Los Angeles, and attended UCLA to study acting. In April 1953, she established residence in Las Vegas for the divorce. Five months later the legal separation papers were signed, and on November 10, Joy filed suit for divorce in superior court, claiming Lance stayed out all night gambling. "When I asked him where he had been, he told me it was none of my business," she told Superior Judge Clarence M. Hanson.

---

7 Source: telephone conversation with author, 03-31-2018.

8 Van Doren, Mamie and Aveilhe, Art. *Playing the Field — Sex, Stardom, Love, and Life in Hollywood.* New Port Beach, CA: Starlet Suave Books, 2013.

Besides his outdoor activities, Joy mentioned that he would bring all sorts of undesirable characters into their home and embarrassed her in front of them. "I used to go downstairs and ask him please to stop gambling, because I had to have some sleep. I had to go to work the next morning. He laughed at me and said he would gamble all he pleased."[9] She asked for no alimony or community property division.

Lance made a name for himself a couple of years later. He appeared as the lead in B-movies like *The Other Woman* (1954) with Cleo Moore, had a part in the science fiction classic *This Island Earth* (1955), and appeared in the cult classics *The She-Creature* (1956) and *Voodoo Woman* (1957), both with Marla English. Joy recalled later, "He was an actor. I paid for his acting lessons, fencing lessons, speech lessons and I don't know what else. But then my money ran out."[10] Adding, "I had to pay for his acting lessons first and there never was any money left to pay for mine. No Hollywood actress, unless she is a big star, can afford an actor for a husband."[11]

Joy enjoyed being single again and was out on the town to play the field. She started dating actor Larry Chance. RKO studio boss and womanizer Howard Hughes also laid his roving eye on her. He took her out on several dates. Larry was not happy with her dating the eccentric movie mogul. "Howard Hughes loved industrial-sized breasts, and the minute he saw Joi, he wanted to possess her. She finally agreed to a date, but her current 'beau,' actor Larry Chance, burst in on their dinner and physically carried her from the restaurant! That ended her almost-relationship with Mr. Hughes…and Mr. Chance."[12]

---

9 *Herald Express*, November 10, 1953.

10 *Tab — The Pocket Picture Magazine*, October 1959.

11 *Utica NY Observer*, March 8, 1959.

12 Hunter, Alexis. *Joi Lansing — A Body to Die For. A Love Story*. Albany: Bear Manor Media, 2015.

Joi in Las Vegas, 1950.

On the set of *Glory Alley*, 1952.

Pier 23, publicity.

The Monroe Comparison

With Marilyn Monroe taking over the crown of Betty Grable at 20th Century Fox, Cleo Moore starring in B-movie potboilers at Columbia and Mamie Van Doren as the new discovery and 'answer to Marilyn Monroe' at Universal, there seemed to be no need to build up the career of another blonde starlet.

To keep her name listed as a promising newcomer, Joy had to appear at premieres, dine with influential producers and make sure she was mentioned in the gossip columns of newspapers and magazines. On July 15, 1953, she attended the premiere of *Stalag 17* in Los Angeles. Columnist Sheilah Graham compared her to the woman she'd lost parts to in her past, and to whom she would be compared with for the rest of her show business career. In the *San Antonio Express* Sheilah wrote, "...but Joy Lansing came alone in an expensive open convertible and stole the show with a Marilyn Monroe wiggle and wardrobe."

Joy didn't dislike Marilyn, for she understood where she was coming from. Both girls started out as starlets at a major studio in the 1940s. In the early 1950s, when Joy's career dwindled, Marilyn held the best cards, renewing her contract at 20th Century Fox and gaining fame through her sexpot parts in several comedies, while Joy was playing chorus girl cameos at the studio that had once groomed her as one of their most promising newcomers. About the Monroe resemblance, Alexis Hunter mentioned, "She was just like Marilyn, very sweet and almost childlike with her innocence. I've never heard negative stuff about her. She had a similar background with MGM…lots of crap! She was an angel and a pure person. Her innocence was never destroyed by the studios."[13]

Apart from the Marilyn Monroe comparison, her resemblance to actresses Lana Turner and Virginia Mayo was still mentioned now and then. Joy had to rethink how she wanted to present herself. In the second half of 1953, Joi decided to reinvent herself by becoming a brunette. A couple of films and an unsold TV pilot testify to this hair color change. Her

---

13 Source: email contact with author.

agent got her a contract for a possible new TV show called *Dixie Dugan*. She was cast to play the title character, a gorgeous showgirl struggling to make a name for herself in Hollywood. Producer Fred Frieberger and writer William Tunberg adapted the story of the comic strip *Dixie Dugan* to television. Alas, the show wasn't sold and never aired on television.

In mid-1953, Joy was cast to appear in *The French Line* (1954). The movie was a star vehicle for Jane Russell, and because of the daring costumes it wasn't released until one year after shooting. Directly after *The French Line*, producer Robert Sparks interviewed 653 girls to select 127 finalists to work in his upcoming movie. *Son of Sinbad* (1955) saw Joy cast as a descendant of Ali Baba's forty thieves. This all girl troupe was led by starlet Joanne Jordan. Among the other raiders were Kim Novak and Dolores Michaels. The latter remembered, "Since we were cast as raiders, we all had the same costumes and wore orange pants, white crepe blouses with cummerbunds, boots and orange headgear."[14] Gloria Pall, who'd met Joy back in 1951, was cast as a harem beauty. "The next time I saw Joy was when we worked in *Son of Sinbad* starring Dale Robertson. There was a huge room filled with topless beauties being made up, in the make-up room. We had to wear lots of make-up under our veiled see-thru costumes. There were about fifty make-up women smearing us with cold sponges. Joy was standing next to me. Her breasts were large and statue like. We giggled as they applied those cold sponges to our firm young bodies."[15] Just like *The French Line*, the release of *Son of Sinbad* was postponed, because of the problems Howard Hughes ran into with the Production Code Office. A November 30, *Hollywood Reporter* news item reported that Joy was cast in Alfred Hitchcock's *Rear Window* (1954). At the beginning of the movie, James Stewart watches a pair of brunette rooftop sunbathers, Stephanie Griffin and Joy. Their part in the picture was so small, that if you blinked, you would have missed them.

Joy's brunette days were short lived. In 1954, she returned to her original flaxen haired persona. She attracted Russell Birdwell to be her publicist. In 1939, he had opened his offices, Russell Birdwell and Associates, in Beverly Hills and New York. Among the many actresses he publicized were Carole Lombard, Marlene Dietrich, Joan Blondell and Jane Russell. Besides Joy, Birdwell also handled clients like Anne Baxter, and starlets Sara Shane and Roberta Haynes. Birdwell publicized Joy as a 'boudoir blonde,' the sultry type. The casting in two movies was the result

---

14 Kleno, Larry. *Kim Novak on Camera*. New York: A.S. Barnes & Company, Inc., 1980.

15 Source: email contact with author.

of his publicity campaign. She was chosen to play a small part in Burt Lancaster's *The Kentuckian* (1955). Filming started in August 1954, near Owensboro, Kentucky. Joy's cameo appearance ended on the cutting room floor. In *Daddy Long Legs* (1955), she is briefly seen in 'The International Playboy' musical number with Fred Astaire. Harrison Carroll described the filming of the scene in his newspaper column. "They are ready to

Candid photo of Joi as a brunette, circa 1953. COURTESY OF JOHN SHUPE

shoot the number now. The playback starts. At a signal from Academy Award winning cameraman Leon Shamroy, the big camera crane moves forward. Astaire starts haughtily down the stairs...At the foot of the stairs, a statuesque brunet, Suzanne Alexander, and a curvaceous blond, Joy Lansing, try to attract Astaire's attention. Six other beauties, among them a stunning blond Jeanne Moorhead, reach out toward him. When he ignores them, they throw themselves face down on the floor and hold up their arms pleadingly toward the retreating figure."[16] Barrie Chase also appeared in the number. "Fred came in and did his number, he didn't really socialize with anybody. Very focused on the work, in and out, you know. There were all showgirls in that number, and there I was. It was hilarious, I never worked with showgirls before, you know. My goodness,

16 *The Day*, February 21, 1955.

all the men would come to visit the showgirls. They were treated like little princesses. Dancers, for some reasons, were the workers. That was a very funny experience."[17] Terry Moore co-starred with Fred Astaire and Leslie Caron. She recalled, "I met Joy on the movie set and she was a lovely, charming girl. We didn't spend anytime offset, so I didn't have the opportunity to get to know her on a personal level. She was very beautiful and seemed to have a delightful personality."[18]

Apart from these two cameo parts and her many appearances on the small screen, Joy had become a semi-regular in the popular Warner Bros. short comedies, *Behind the Eight Ball*. The series involved 'Mister Average' Joe McDoakes, an anti-hero played by George O'Hanlon. Joy was cast to play the beautiful blonde who baffles Joe. In total she appeared in five movies in featured and walk-on parts. In her first appearance on the series, we see her as the glamorous Lorna Lamour. In *So You Want to Go to a Nightclub* (1954), Joe's wife (Jane Frazee) persuades Joe to visit a nightclub with her. Joe grumbles that he finds dining out way too expensive, but when he is introduced to Lorna he orders champagne and insists on paying the bill. Of course, he can't afford it and when Lorna and her beau come to visit the nightclub several days later, we see Joe working as a waiter and his wife as a cigarette girl. In *So You're Taking in a Roomer* (1954), Joy's part is much smaller. She sports a new, short haircut and plays a sexy lodger. When director Richard L. Bare needed a sexy secretary for *So You Want to Be a V.P.* (1955), Joy was called upon to play Miss Pointdexter, a girl who wears her sweaters a couple of sizes too small. In *So You Want to Be a Policeman* (1955) Joy's character had no name to go by. She's seen as a beautiful blonde, driving around town and getting a ticket from policeman Joe McDoakes.

With movie roles at a minimum, television seemed the medium where Joy could profile herself. She teamed up with comedian Jack Benny in the TV movie, *The Face is Familiar*. *The Independent Press Telegram* mentioned, "There's a full four-minute pantomime in which Benny appears with a couple of beautiful girls (Joy Lansing and Jean Willes) who delightfully resemble Marilyn Monroe and Ava Gardner." The Monroe tag proved to be hard to get rid of, and soon she was mentioned in TV guides as 'TV's answer to Marilyn Monroe.'

In January 1955, Joy's appearance on *The Bob Cummings Show* showed her in the opening scene of the show called "Calling Doctor Baxter," as a

---

17 Source: telephone conversation with author, 03-31-2018.

18 Source: email contact with author.

bridal model being attacked by a gorilla (photographer Bob Cumming's secretary Schultzy in disguise). It was the first of many TV series that year. Joy decided that a new name seemed appropriate; although it was a subtle change this time. Joy became Joi Lansing. In a 1961 interview she recalled, "I've changed it to Joi five years ago, so it would look better in print. You know, it changed my whole luck. I started getting parts immediately."

On March 23, Joi signed a freelance contract with RKO studios and directly flew to Mexico to start filming *The Boy and the Bull*.[19] The story of the movie is about a little boy and his bull, Gitano. When the bull is sold and brought to Mexico City to appear in bull fights, the boy travels to Mexico City to be with his beloved friend. Joi played an American actress travelling the country with Rodolfo Hoyos and matador Carlos Navarro. She's being educated about the bull fighting game by Rodolfo and has her eyes on Carlos for a little romance. Joi's scenes are brief, and she doesn't have a lot of speaking lines. She's important to the story as the outside view on the cruelty of bullfighting. Joi looked extremely beautiful in her scenes which were photographed by Jack Cardiff. Michel Ray, nowadays known as Michel De Carvalho, played the young boy. Michel doesn't remember working with Joi, but he does remember how much fun he had shooting the movie. "I have no actual recollection of the director or any of the other actors. I was a mere child with a bunch of grown-ups. I do remember the young bulls being fun to play with, and most of all I remember with fun the Mexico City scenes, from running in the streets to the ride in the motorcycle side car. No doubles in those days. Every time I go back to Mexico City I still have fond memories."[20] Joi filmed in and around Mexico City for a month. Every time she walked down the street she gathered crowds. "It was like being the Pied Piper and wonderful for my ego," Joi told the press on her return to the United States.

Back in Hollywood, producer Max Schnabel contracted Joi for a starring part in his stage play, *The Bride Wore Blue*. Set in New York, the plot featured a murder and the mystery surrounding it. On August 17, *The Los Angeles Times* mentioned that actor John Lupton was to join the cast. The

---

19 The movie was released as *The Brave One*. Screenwriter Robert Rich won the Oscar for Best Motion Picture Story. Robert Rich was a front for screen writer Dalton Trumbo during the period of his being blacklisted during the McCarthy era. When Trumbo appeared before a Congressional committee and was threatened with a Contempt of Congress citation for not answering questions, he told the committee that that would be appropriate, since he had nothing but contempt for them.

20 Source: email contact with author.

production was to be launched on the West Coast, in Autumn. When Joi decided not to go through with the play, actress Patti Gallagher was offered the part. However, the play never saw the light of day. Instead of starring in a stage play, Joi wanted nothing more than to be the star in a motion picture. She auditioned for a part in Paul Newman's *Somebody Up There Likes Me* (1956) at MGM. The screen test led to nothing. Back

Joy and Virginia with relatives from the Rice family, 1954. COURTESY OF JOHN SHUPE

on poverty row, she played a gang moll in Republic's *Terror at Midnight* (1956). Filming started late November 1955. Although Joi was not listed on the movie's casting list, she got some good exposure dressed in a black slinky dress, while delivering a few catchy lines.

The *San Mateo Times* dedicated a small piece about Joi under the title "TV has its answer for Marilyn Monroe."[21] Reporter Bob Foster wrote about Joy's appearance on the *Four Star Playhouse*: "Last Thursday night however, Charles Boyer came up with a half-hour effort which in itself was not the greatest to come out of the series. But, we suppose Boyer in this one was to be excused. After all, he was presenting to American TViewers one of the most beautiful specimens of blonde loveliness to

---

21 November 14, 1955.

come along since Marilyn Monroe posed for that now famous picture. The young lady in question is a blonde by the name Joi Lansing, and she was featured with Boyer in 'The Devil to Pay.' In the early portions of the drama the young lady wore her hair in a severe and unglamorous bun. This was while she was playing secretary to Boyer. Boyer portrayed the role of a hard-hearted businessman. In the final portions of the show, Miss Lansing was shown as the ravishing blonde beauty she is."

In an episode for *The Ford Television Theatre* called "A Smattering of Bliss," Joi played the part of glamorous actress Inez Hamilton. It starred Larry Parks and Betty Garrett, a Hollywood husband-wife writing team who have success in writing but not in marriage, especially after the leading lady in their plays makes a play for the husband. Larry is smitten with Joi, making his wife concerned and a bit jealous of the voluptuous dumb blonde. Joi clearly acted with Marilyn Monroe in mind, the breathy voice, the come-hither looks. She looked marvellous and handled her lines well. In reply to Betty's sarcasm and bitchy comments, Joi answers, "Maybe I'm dumb, but at least I'm direct. I say what's on my mind, it saves time. If there was somebody after my man, I'd tell her to lay off." Later, Betty confesses to a friend that she wrote these lines for Joi to say. In return for her husband, Betty promised the blonde seductress to write a good part in a new script. One review stated that the teleplay, "…is being touted as one of the funniest shows ever. Joi Lansing, TV's newest blonde doll, is featured."[22]

Joi appeared in the popular Joe McDoakes series one more time. In *So You Think the Grass is Greener* (1956), Joe dreams of a life with a girl as sweet as his colleague, Miss Backspace. He visualizes her in their office wearing nothing more than a bathing suit. The Devil makes him a proposition: to switch his nagging wife for the lovely blonde. But soon Joe finds out that Geraldine Backspace sleeps in, leaving him to make breakfast for her. She doesn't clean the house and when Joe's out to work, she invites the milkman, postman and the delivery boy in, all at the same time! This appearance was quite out of character for Joi, who usually played the sweet, dumb blonde.

On January 15, 1956, *The Ogden Standard-Examiner* mentioned that Joi's uncle and aunt, together with their son John Jr. and grandparents, had visited Joi and her mother. John, his father Raymond and Joi made a trip to Disneyland. "The day was magical to me. Joi went with my father and me. I think Disneyland was in its second year and we had so much fun!

---

22 *Long Island City NY Star Journal*, November 1955.

Joi was so impressed with everything, she was like a kid herself and being such a beauty drew a lot of attention from others in the crowd. Other outings we did together were water skiing on Bear Lake in Northern Utah. She and I used to love shopping for clothing for her in downtown Ogden. She said most of her clothing was purchased from stores in downtown Ogden. She thought the dresses, sweaters, coats and shoes were her favorite styles. Her favorite perfume at that time was April Violets. She liked going to the monastery up Ogden Canyon. They have and had a gift shop where she would purchase honey to take back to California."[23] Joi's brother Larry wasn't at Disneyland that day; he probably stayed with his father at the time. If the fact that Joi was eleven years older than Larry, and them having different fathers, meant that they were not that close is not to be said with certainty. John was not aware of them having any problems between them. Therefore, he had no way of comparing who between Larry and himself was the closer. "I don't remember being with Joi and Larry at the same time more than once or twice. I don't know much about their personal relationships. I do remember a period of time when Larry was living at home with his mother. He was in high school; Joi was on her own with her own residence. I know my dad and grandfather provided some financial support to both Joi and Larry. I think they didn't show any favoritism, so I don't think that caused any tensions between them. I know Joi hung on to the money she eventually received when our grandpa died. She still had the full amount locked away at the time of her death. From what I heard Larry made use of that money rather quickly. They had each received the same amount as I did."[24]

Joi's mother was now married to multi-millionaire Carlton Wasmansdorff, who owned a citrus ranch in Santa Paula, California.[25] John Shupe remembers Carlton as a friendly and wonderful uncle. Virginia, as Alexis recalls, was married to Carlton only for his money. She couldn't stand her husband and expressed how much she wanted to get rid of him behind his back. Unlike her mother, Joi worked hard to provide a steady income for herself. For the last three years, she had been in front of TV cameras almost constantly and pulled down a steady income of $500 to $1000 a week. This was quite a lot of money for a freelance actress at the time.

23 Source: email contact with author.

24 Source: email contact with author.

25 Carlton Wasmansdorff was born in Montana on June 2, 1904. He was married three times. From his first marriage he has one son, Richard, who was born in 1930.

Joy as a brunette, 1953. COURTESY OF ALEXIS HUNTER

TV's busiest blonde, 1954.

Still from unknown TV show, 1954.

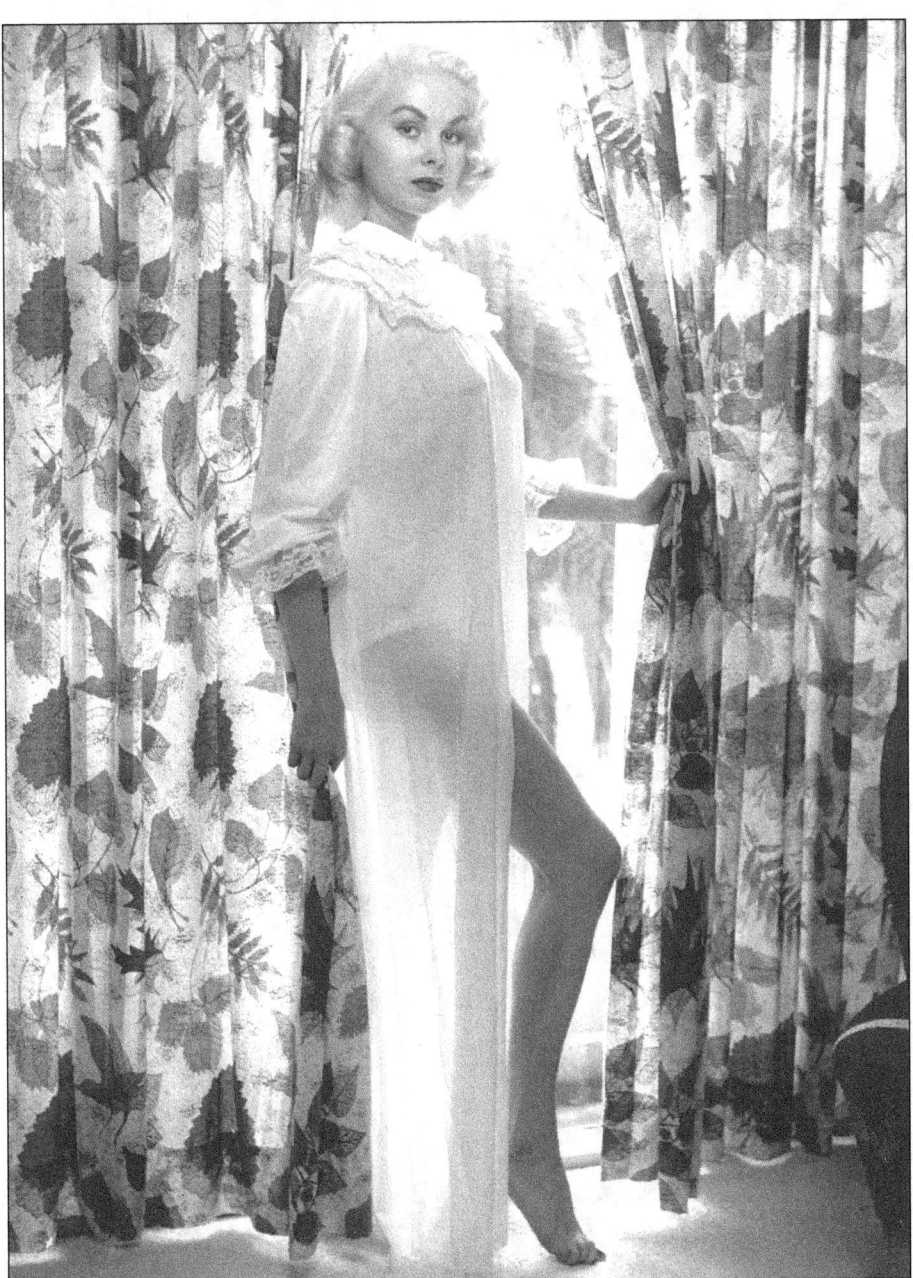

The Boudoir Blonde, 1954.

86 "WHEN A GIRL'S BEAUTIFUL"

So You Want to Go to a Nightclub, with Jane Frazee, Del Moore and George O'Hanlon, 1954.

The Brave One, 1955.

Publicity photo for *A Smattering of Bliss*, 1955.

Love That Joi!

In November 1955, Joi's casting in a new TV show proved to be the restart her career needed. The show's creator, producer and head writer Paul Henning spotted Joi when she was attending drama classes at UCLA. He liked what he saw and signed her to a contract. Joi played Shirley Swanson, a model chasing photographer Bob Cummings. Her part in *The Bob Cummings Show* required more than just looking good. Bob demanded a strict working ethic from his co-stars. He stressed in an interview that besides being beautiful the girls on his show needed other qualities. "Don't get me wrong; physical beauty is definitely necessary, but that's only the base from which to work. Versatility heads the list where we're concerned. A girl should have the capacity to produce a wide range of expressions to suit the mood of what we're trying to catch in the scene. Our show is rehearsed and filmed on a strict daily time limit, so you can see how important it is for all concerned to know just exactly what they're supposed to do whenever the camera is aimed at them. For example, Joi Lansing is a girl who can look wholesome and fetching in a house-dress at an ironing board, yet fall into a completely different mood for a glamour shot in a tight-fitting costume. In other words, she doesn't rely on a change of costume to capture the mood; her emotions are elastic enough to feel the idea and put it across to the camera."[26]

Joi's character Shirley was usually found in Bob's arms when Schultzy, the secretary, tried to find out what is developing in her boss' darkroom. "I kiss Bob with zoom but always with tenderness. That's what women like," Joi emphasized in an interview. "Bob knows that he can always get men to watch his TV show by filling it with pretty girls, but it takes women viewers to keep those old ratings up. Don't forget, it's either Mama or the teen-age daughter who answers the phone first."[27] Dwayne Hickman played Chuck. He was impressed by Joi's beauty, but she showed no interested in him at all. He was the young guy on the set. He recalls, "Bob Cummings was

26 *The Salt Lake Tribune*, October 12, 1958.

27 *Utica NY Observer*, March 8, 1959.

always polite and professional. He would flirt with the models exactly as his character, Bob Collins, nothing suggestive or out of line. Bob was the consummate professional. Hours of rehearsals, lines always learned, timing exact and he/we would work on a scene until it was perfect."[28]

The Bob Cummings Show — aka *Love That Bob!* — was filmed in one day with no live audience. Call time was 6 a.m. A work day was 10-12

The Bob Cummings Show, "The Models Revolt," 1957.

hours during the week. In the weekend, there was no filming. To make sure all scenes were shot on Friday, the actors often worked late that day. Between rehearsal, Joi and the rest of the crew sat around waiting for the lights to be set up and last-minute changes in the script meant extra rehearsing of the new lines. Paul Henning's wife Ruth recalled, "The show was done in a radically different way — keeping it all in the family, so to speak. Paul would produce and write. Bob would star and eventually direct. They would use two cameras shooting from different locations, thereby eliminating the need for constant repetitions of shots to get new angles and close-ups. What's more, they had plenty of rehearsal and shot it in one day. Very economical."[29]

28 Source: email contact with author.

29 Henning, Ruth. *The First Beverly Hillbilly — The Untold Story of the Creator of Rural TV Comedy*. Kansas City: Woodneath Press, 2017.

Joi's work on the show payed her $400 a week; money she invested in her career. She refined her acting by taking drama lessons, went to the gym every other day and got vocal lessons from vocal coach Harriet Lee. Harriet had worked with Joi earlier when she was under contract to MGM. She recognized Joi's talents and supported her vocal ambitions. In 1957, Joi said in an interview, "I have an excellent teacher and sing daily into a tape recorder. Someone heard me sing and flipped!" That 'someone' could have been an executive of the small REO label. Joi recorded a 45 r.p.m. single for them, with the two songs "Love Me/What's It Gonna Be." The record received very little airplay and failed to chart.

Joi and Larry, 1955.
COURTESY OF JOHN SHUPE

Just one stage over from *The Bob Cummings Show*, *The Adventures of Ozzie and Harriet* was filmed. And, since Bob Cummings played a photographer constantly in search of models, what could be more natural than for some of the choicer tidbits to appear on both shows. Ozzie Nelson used to slip into the Cummings rehearsals to cast his own show. He commented, "I noticed that when we started shooting with attractive girls, more people came to watch the show. Thanks to girls like Joi Lansing, Ingrid Goude and Carol Morris and the rest, we're beginning to see our old friends again."[30] Unlike *The Bob Cummings Show*, *The Adventures of Ozzie and Harriet* was filmed with a live audience. Joi became a semi regular on the show, appearing approximately once a year, between 1956 and 1963. The popular show stopped in 1966, in its fourteenth season. Asked about the difference in acting in movies or television, Joi answered, "I work in television as much as I do in pictures — and don't let anyone tell you that TV isn't twice as hard. The mediums are nowhere near alike, even the filmed TV shows. But the 'live' shows are the hardest. If you ask me, live TV is the most difficult and demanding medium in the entertainment field. But you learn plenty and you earn it fast!"[31]

30 *Albany N.Y. Sunday Times Union*, June 30, 1957.

31 *Los Angeles Examiner*, February 26, 1956.

Joi had become a hot property, and cinema goers didn't have to wait long to see Joi on the big screen. She was the leading lady in the action movie *Hot Cars*. Filmed in March, Joi gave a good performance as bad girl Karen Winter. Although her screen time is limited, and the movie was made on a low budget, Joi had the chance to escape her dumb blonde character. She only has a couple of scenes but is captivating in each one

Joi at her grandparent's house, 1956. COURTESY OF JOHN SHUPE

of them. The scene that really shows off her beauty is the one where she's sleeping and the ringing of the telephone wakes her up. She's clearly naked between the sheets.

The press wasn't impressed with the movie nor the cast. One review read in part, "John Bromfield looks earnest, and the girl who first lures him into illegal time wasting, Joi Lansing, looks like forty other Hollywood

Hot Cars, with John Bromfield, 1956.

blondes. The picture keeps going, and, if you haven't a better place to go, you can pay attention without an acute sense of wrong doing yourself."[32] Being judged as "just another blonde" was painful for Joi. She wondered why well-stacked blondes were compared to each other and sexy brunettes and redheads weren't. Nonetheless, the year 1956 glorified the blonde bombshell, and Joi decided to take advantage of the platinum sexbomb hype. Several girls had made their mark already. Jayne Mansfield had been a smash hit on Broadway and was now making headlines with her contract at 20th Century Fox. British Diana Dors was imported by RKO to appear in two movies. Kim Novak was on the rise at Columbia, and Mamie Van Doren was released from her Universal contract and did very well on her own. Although Joi didn't have a studio contract, television

32 New York Post, August 9, 1956.

gave her plenty of opportunities to show off her beauty and talent. Her work on *The Bob Cummings Show* kept her in the spotlight and Lucille Ball and Desi Arnaz had made her an offer to appear in several of their productions.

When Desilu produced a pilot for a possible new TV series with Orson Welles, Joi was contracted for the leading part. Filming commenced on

The Fountain of Youth, 1956.

May 8. The shooting was planned to take five days, but Welles expanded the schedule into a six-week production. Welles introduced each short movie himself. In *The Fountain of Youth,* Joi was seen as the vain 1920s actress and society girl Carolyn Coates. Dan Tobin played a respected scientist, an expert in the field of human glands. When the aging Dan falls for the young Broadway actress, he is quite surprised that she falls in love with him too. After a three-year absence in Vienna, where he has been conducting secret research, Dan returns to the United States. He learns that Joi has left him for a handsome tennis player, Rick Jason. The scientist plans to take revenge, by making a potion that promises eternal youth. Swallowing his anger, Dan invites the couple to his laboratory, after they return from their honeymoon. He presents them a tube with the magical serum. Joi and Rick plan to divide it in half but are told that only drinking the entire vial is effective. In this way, Dan hopes to split the couple, which is effectively shown in the second half of the episode. Orson Welles gave Joi the opportunity to show she could act. She's especially effective in the scene where she stands before the mirror and sees herself growing old and is horrified by the sight.

Joi had a happy time working with Orson. "Oh, he was wonderful. I couldn't recognize myself. Also, Orson gave me confidence. You wouldn't believe it, but I need confidence."[33] Supervising editor Dann Cahn recalled that Orson also enjoyed Joi's company very much. "I could tell you specifics about a couple of events in the projection room. I leave it to your imagination." Rick Jason remembered, "My two co-stars were Joi Lansing, a woman who played dumb bleached blondes, and was anything but dumb or blonde, and Dan Tobin, a fine character comedian. Dan, the eldest of we three, passed away in 1982. Poor Joi, who was a true joy to work with, died in her early thirties, cutting short a promising career. There was a three-shot resembling the marriage ceremony in which Dan, standing in the position of the preacher, makes us promise to keep a secret. We were set in place and said our lines as the camera moved around us a full 360 degrees. Welles and his cameraman walked around this triangle as we rehearsed, talking *sotto voce*. When we got to the end of the scene he'd say, "Good, run it again," and we'd run it again, and again. And again. After half-an-hour of rehearsing and standing in one spot without moving, Orson said to do it once more. "Orson," I said, "we've been standing here for thirty minutes. You've heard of tired?" "You're right," he said. He indicated three bent cane-backed chairs and asked for them to be brought into the set. "My God," I thought, "the man has some humanity in him after all." "Turn the chairs around," he directed, "now then, people, rest your hands on the chair backs and let's do it one more time." Alfred Hitchcock once protested, when told he'd referred to actors as cattle, "I never said actors were cattle. I said actors should be *treated* like cattle." That's about the way Welles treated his actors."[34]

Another Desilu production Joi appeared in, caused a lot of tension between Lucille Ball and husband Desi Arnaz. Besides being a heavy drinker, Desi was a womanizer, which gave Lucille plenty of heartache. While filming an episode for the popular series *I Love Lucy*, there was reportedly lots of sexual tension between Joi and Desi. Child actor Richard Keith, whose real name is Keith Thibodeaux, played little Ricky on the episode "Desert Island." He recalls, "I also remember watching

---

33 *The Charleston Gazette*, June 13, 1957.

34 *www.scrapbooksofmymind.com*

the chemistry between Joi Lansing and Desi, and Lucy's reaction. Even at my age, I knew this couldn't be good." Joi however kept professional and kept Desi at a friendly distance. About Joi, Thibodeaux remembers, "My memory of her was a nice, very pretty lady who was very friendly. Desi and Lucy were naturally a very passionate couple with a lot of tension around them. I'm sure Joi exacerbated it as Desi had a reputation for beautiful girls and a Latin charm. I enjoyed working on that episode."[35]

A rather peculiar story about Joi appeared in the *San Mateo Times* of July 21. The media reporter for the newspaper, Bob Foster covered local radio and television for more than forty years. Covering everyone from local disc jockeys to Hollywood stars, he was a respected and trusted columnist known for his gregarious nature. Interested in Joi, he opened the half page article asking, "Does anybody know where Joi Lansing can be found?" Impressed with her appearance and TV work, Foster stated that she could compete with Marilyn Monroe and Diana Dors with no fear. He expressed his amazement that he could not track her down for an interview.

A person who did get the chance to meet Joi was Wesley L. Fox, a now retired Colonel in the United States Marine Corps, who received the Medal of Honor for his actions during the Vietnam War. At the time, the twenty-four-year-old Sgt. Fox got his photo in the papers embracing Joi. In his memoires, he recalled the meeting. "Colonel Henry P. (Jim) Crowe, the base Chief of Staff, provided some duties not covered by DI School. The premier of *Hold Back the Night*, [July 29, 1956] a Korean War movie starring William Holden, was to take place in Oceanside. In addition to showing the movie, Camp Pendleton's Commanding General invited Hollywood down for an Open House and an all-day Dog and Pony show. Among the movie stars were two young starlets who would have personal escorts and be given the red-carpet treatment. I reported in khakis and carried my blues for the evening affair. Pendleton assigned a corporal to escort Cleo Moore; my starlet was Joi Lansing. We were a foursome for the entire day and evening. This was my first time with a celebrity or as part of a special group, and it was pure enjoyment. I played the role, and Joi and I hit it off well. She invited me to her place in Hollywood two weeks later."[36]

One should not make an idle invitation to a Marine; Mister Fox kept his date. "She invited me up to Hollywood, and she would show me the

---

35 Source: email contact with author.

36 Col. Wesley L. Fox. *Marine Rifleman — Forty-Three Years in the Corps*. US: Potomac Books, Inc., 2002.

movie world. I had Drill Instructor duty every other weekend, so I allowed that I would like to accept for the Saturday two weeks away. She agreed and gave me her address. Of course, that was a big event for me, and I did much bragging among my fellow drill instructors at San Diego about what I had coming. It never dawned on me to confirm with a phone call. As I write in my memoir, she had a surprised look on her face as she opened her door to me. She was in a bathing suit and cleaning her apartment. She was embarrassed and allowed that she had forgotten our plan for the day. But she quickly recovered with how we would make the day work."³⁷ First, Joi took Wesley to her mother's home, then to a male friend's apartment to cancel their evening plans. Cancelling the date with her boyfriend that evening really impressed the sergeant with what Joi thought of him. A sightseeing tour of Hollywood followed, including a walk through some movie studios and lunch in a place well above his pay grade. "We walked, looked, and talked, and I got the picture. Joi was repaying me for what I had done for her. She also helped me see that I wanted no part of her lifestyle. Joi convinced me that there were no real men in Hollywood, including John Wayne; she related a personal experience with my Hollywood hero that would not help sell movie tickets. According to her, Hollywood males had no respect for females, and again Wayne received the brunt of her criticism. I enjoyed a full day in Hollywood but was relieved to be southbound on 101 later that night.³⁸

With Wesley L. Fox, July 1956.

"As to John Wayne, she grouped him with other Hollywood male stars with wanting nothing from women but sex. She was really blistering with her words regarding their actions and conduct with women. Joi responded to my statement that John Wayne was my favorite actor. She stated that

---

37 Source: email contact with author.

38 Col. Wesley L. Fox. *Marine Rifleman — Forty-Three Years in the Corps*. US: Potomac Books, Inc., 2002.

Wayne was just like the other male actors in Hollywood, interested in women only for sex and treated women just that way, use them and move on. She had no time for Wayne, with our discussion or otherwise and she dropped the subject. It was obvious to me that she disliked him, but she didn't get into it."[39] Gossip journalist Louella Parsons, who covered the premiere in her newspaper column, accused Joi of bad taste. She wrote, "If spanking young ladies hadn't gone out of style — or is against the law? — I'd like to take a good old-fashioned paddle to Joi Lansing for that dress she wore to the USO benefit premiere of *Hold Back the Night* for the Marines at Camp Pendleton. I hope other starlets or near-stars will take a good look and know what not to wear when appearing at an armed forces base." Parsons continued, "If Joi selected this dress to wear on such an occasion, she's guilty of very bad taste. If she was told to wear it under the mistaken idea that the near-nudity is 'glamorous,' she was very badly advised and should listen to somebody else instead."[40] Of course Sgt. Fox didn't complain about Joi's choice in clothes.

Meanwhile journalist Bob Foster hadn't given up on getting in contact with Joi, and in October, he finally met the actress he had longed for to interview. "Last week-end, we ventured to Hollywood for a couple of days and were mentioning that it was rather unusual that Miss Lansing couldn't be contacted for an interview. Sitting nearby, with his back turned to us, was an old friend, Tony Remineh…it also seems that Tony handled Miss Lansing's publicity not too long ago. Anyway, he walked over and said, 'I can get you together with the lady.' A couple of telephone calls later, we were on our way. We found, as we expected, that Miss Lansing was quite a dish. A most unusual dish, in fact. She is very blonde, beautiful and has a mighty good head on her pretty shoulders." Bob concluded his article, "It would appear that Miss Lansing is headed for bigger things. She has a couple of feature pictures on the hook and is still scheduled for a number of television films."[41]

On October 26, Joi attended the premiere of *The Brave One*. Reviews for the movie were harsh. The *New York Times* held the story as childish and sentimental, adding a positive note on the photography in color and Cinemascope, done by well known and respected English photographer Jack Cardiff.[42] *Variety* mentioned Joi in its review. Once again Joi was

---

39 Source: email contact with author.

40 *Modern Screen*, November 1956.

41 *San Mateo Times*, October 13, 1956.

42 Jack Cardiff (1914-2009) also photographed Marilyn Monroe for *The Prince and the Showgirl* (1957).

rated by her looks rather than her acting abilities. "The only cash value here is the possibility of ad and lobby art using Joi Lansing, a well filled-out blonde."

Another B-movie, *Hot Shots*, was a late entry of the successful Bowery Boys series. It saw Joi as the sexy secretary of comedian Huntz Hall and straight guy Stanley Clements. The boys have been hired by a TV net-

Hot Shots, 1956.

work to keep their star attraction, little Joey Evans, in line. Joi seems a sweet innocent secretary, but she's the moll and accomplice of the double-crossing uncle/manager of the boy. Together with her lover and his gang she plans to kidnap the boy for ransom. Of course, the Bowery Boys come to the rescue and Joi's character is arrested by the police. *Hot Shots* was released on December 23. Joi was mentioned in one review. "Phil Phillips, playing the boy star, is a smart addition to the company. Joi

Lansing provides light romantic interest, as a secretary. Robert Shayne, Mark Dana, Queenie Smith, David Condon and Jimmy Murphy make good aides for Huntz and Stanley."[43]

On February 18, 1957, Orson Welles started shooting *Touch of Evil* (1958) for Universal. Exactly one month later he filmed the opening shot of the film. Orson wanted Joi for the part of stripper Zita. Filming took place in Venice, a suburb of Los Angeles. Joi is seen in a car with a man, crossing the border to Mexico. The shadow of the windshield frame is across her face. She complains about the ticking she keeps hearing. A couple of minutes later the car drives away and suddenly explodes. Apart from some of her earliest bit parts, this must have been the shortest time she was seen on film. Joi felt frustrated about the parts that were offered to her and the postponed premieres of some of her movies and TV shows. Her ten years in Hollywood had known times of recognition, but that didn't seem to have helped her to pass the threshold of fame. She judged that her looks were standing in the way of a successful career. "I'm the sweet, dumb, curvy blonde type and I want to do more than that. But look at these round cheeks — they're like a chipmunk's. No character. How am I going to get good parts with this baby face? Maybe I'll have to wait five years for some wrinkles."[44]

---

43 *Buffalo-Courier Express,* April 15, 1957.

44 *The Charleston Gazette,* June 13, 1957

Publicity for *Touch of Evil*, 1957.

Sinatra's Girl

In December 1957, "Bob, the Gunslinger," an episode of *The Bob Cummings Show*, aired and earned Joi a positive review. It was based on her appearance instead of her acting but was flattering nevertheless. "Everyone on the show seems to be having romantic dreams, and who can blame them! Prominent among the attractions is Joi Lansing. Outstanding performer is Joi Lansing. Prettiest performer is Joi Lansing. Not recommended for males unless they have an air conditioner nearby."[45] It was Bob who introduced Joi to vitamin pills and weightlifting. "Bob was the person who got me to take vitamins. When I first met him I said, 'I didn't know Bob Cummings had a son.' It was Bob himself, but he looked that young. I thought if vitamins could do that much for Bob, they surely could do something for me, too."[46] In her remarks on the subject of weightlifting, her press agent advised her to add, "It develops the bust, cushions the hips, and slims down the waist." It's questionable if Joi's 38-23-25 figure needed any improvement.

In December Joi reported to stage 22 on the Warner Bros. studio lot, to appear in an episode of TV's *Sugarfoot*. In the mid-1950's, the studio had a stable of television westerns. One of the lightest-hearted of the group was *Sugarfoot*, starring Will Hutchins as wannabe lawyer Tom Brewster. A 'sugarfoot' in western terminology is not a flattering thing to be. It implies a person one step below tenderfoot, and a tenderfoot is a greenhorn at everything. The show was an hour in length. It took six days to shoot one episode. In "Bullet Proof," Sugarfoot tricks a gang into believing that he knows the location of the loot from their last bank robbery. Joi held an important part as the female lead, the unsavory but attractive Peaches, who claims to be a belle from Georgia. Gregory Walcott played Peaches' presumed fiancé. The star of the show, Will Hutchins, had made his debut in another TV show in which Joi also appeared. "Joi Lansing! Hot Dog — what a gorgeous gal. I worked with her on two TV shows at

---

45 *Herald Statesman*, Yonkers, N.Y., December 10, 1957.

46 *The Ogden Standard-Examiner*, June 3, 1962.

Warner Bros., circa 1956-1957. One, 'The Magic Brew,' was my *de facto* screen test on the anthology show *Conflict*. As I recall, she was a lovely small-town citizen. Jim Backus and daughter, Dani Crayne, bilked the townsfolks, selling snake oil. On *Sugarfoot's* first season Joi played a femme fatale, Peaches, using most of her wiles to get me to reveal where all the money was hidden. Joi was a joy to work with, not an ounce of ego raised

Left: Joi with Larry's girlfriend Janey at his graduation day, June 1958. COURTESY OF JOHN SHUPE *Right:* Joy and Ray 'Grampy' Shupe, Christmas 1959. COURTESY OF BEVERLY WATKINS

its ugly head, only her beautiful head, body and soul. I didn't have to act, I was mister gaga over Joi Lansing. In the last scene, someone gives me a bag of peaches. 'No thank you!' But her magic gives me the oomph to perform my best mount and ride-off of that season."[47] One review about the particular episode read, "Normally, the mere presence of Joi Lansing in a TV show is enough to earn it a recommendation. Tonight, however, she isn't merely appearing, she's acting."[48]

Several other television shows gave Joi a chance to act too. In popular shows like *Mike Hammer*, *Adventures of Superman* and *Maverick*, she's a substantial part of the episode's story line. In February, *The Frank Sinatra Show* was broadcasted. Joi appeared with Frank and Van Johnson in a

---

47 Source: mail contact with author.

48 *TV Key Previews*, January 21, 1958.

sketch. TV critics mentioned, "Guest Van Johnson 'writes' a play for Frankie and himself. Not much of a sketch, but it has a few laughs and Joi Lansing."[49] Frank hated rehearsing and tried to make eleven shows in fifteen days; the series subsequently received a critical mauling and was Frank's last attempt at a television series. Reviews were harsh, but Joi managed to get a positive notice. "Frank adds some distractions to his crooning tonight in the form of a bevy of beautiful babes who provide a background for his numbers, Van Johnson tries to add a little humor via a sketch...but the effort's biggest asset is the appearance of Joi Lansing."[50]

John Shupe recalls a wonderful day he spent with his cousin in the Summer of 1958. She took him around town and brought him to the studio to meet many celebrities. "She and I spent a day at Warner Bros. Studios, where she took me around to meet several of her favorite people such as Ricky Nelson and Dean Martin. They were on the set filming the movie *Rio Bravo*. We also visited with Will Hutchins filming an episode of *Sugarfoot*. We also talked with Jack Kelly, who played Brett Maverick in the *Maverick* TV Series. The highlight of the Warner Bros. visit was when Ricky Nelson invited Joi and me to join him for lunch at a nearby restaurant (off lot) and he drove us in his beautiful convertible with the top down. Any time Joi and I spent together was truly quality time. She was so special with a beautiful personality!"[51]

In September, *The Fountain of Youth* was finally shown on television. It earned many positive reviews. One read in part, "Onetime boy-genius Orson Welles hasn't lost his touch. This is as witty and imaginative a TV film as we've ever seen. Unlike most films for TV, this one indicates taste, care, intelligence, and a sense of humor. The performances of Dan Tobin, Joi Lansing and Rick Jason as the leads, plus those of everybody else, are superb."[52] *The Fountain of Youth* became the only unsold pilot in television history to win a Peabody Award. The jury mentioned that Welles used narration, stills, live-action and minimal sets to great advantage. The daring camera and editing techniques had rarely been seen in television.

Throughout 1958, Joi moved back and forth between television shows and feature films. Allied Artists hired Joi to make a cameo appearance in *Queen of Outer Space* (1958). Joi was the only girl in the picture that was

---

49 *Peekskill Evening Star*, February 28, 1958.

50 *Long Island Star-Journal*, February 28, 1958.

51 Source: email contact with author.

52 *Niagara Falls Gazette*, September 16, 1958.

not a Venusian. She was cast as the girlfriend of one of the astronauts and bids him farewell before he takes off for the planet Venus. The cult-classic starred Zsa Zsa Gabor, who revolts against the evil queen, Laurie Mitchell. Laurie remembered meeting Joi on the set, "We weren't too friendly. It was 'hello' and 'nice to meet you.' She was absolutely beautiful. Very, very pretty."[53]

Lisa Davis wasn't on the set the day Joi shot her scene with her husband, Patrick Waltz. She does recall working together on *The Bob Cummings Show* in an episode called "Bob and Harvey Get Ambushed." She remembers Joi as, "Cold, not at all friendly and remote." Adding, "I worked with her several times. She just hadn't anything to say. You know, she was professional, that was fine. She did her thing, she knew her lines. She just wasn't someone you got to know. She was just cold and never smiled. She just kept to herself. And that was fine, you know, it was just the way she was." Lisa witnessed Joi being pranked while filming *The Bob Cummings Show*. "Joi padded her bra with falsies. We all knew this and when somebody on the set stuck a safety pin in the side of her padding, she went around with it until she finally noticed the prank. She always denied that she padded her boobs. She wore many, many, we used to call them falsies then. Foam rubber, that's what she wore to make her boobs look larger. One of the actors on the show stuck a safety pin in the side of her, where she couldn't see it."[54]

Joi signed a contract with Frank Capra Productions, Inc. to work on *A Hole in the Head* (1959) for two weeks. She received a salary of $750 per week. She started filming on November 8, in Miami. Originally, Frank had wanted to cast actress Barbara Nichols for the part. In 1957, after working with Barbara in *Pal Joey*, he had told the Morris Agency to recruit her once the production commenced. But after working with Joi on his TV show, he changed his mind. Joi was cast as Keenan Wynn's girlfriend, and she got little more to do than admonish the former for dropping cigar ash on her.

Director Frank Capra recalled how he asked the help of Keenan and Joi in a scene, where Frank flunked his performance with every take. He told them, "Keenan, I want to try something without rehearsing it with Frank. Change your cues, mix up your lines. Joi! Interrupt Frank during his speeches, but keep the scene going, no matter what Frank does. I want

---

53 Source: telephone conversation with author, 10-29-2017.

54 Lisa also worked with Joi on *The Gale Storm Show* (1957). Source: telephone conversation with author, 07-27-2018.

it to be all new for him."⁵⁵ The acting talents of Keenan and Joi helped Frank to stay focused in the scene and it got the best out of him. About working with Frank, Joi said, "One day I saw Frank with a script cutting things out. I said, 'What are you doing?' He said, 'I'm cutting things out. I want to go home.' He got a whim."⁵⁶ Child actor Eddie Hodges played Frank's son. "I was walking by Mr. Sinatra's dressing room and saw a

Joi with several family members. COURTESY OF BEVERLY WATKINS

pretty lady standing there talking with him. He saw me and called me over. He introduced me, saying, 'This is my friend Joi Lansing. Joi, this is Eddie Hodges — he plays my son, Ally." Mr. Sinatra always treated me as an adult and fellow actor, and I always tried to act accordingly. I shook Miss Lansing's hand and told her it was nice meeting her. She was a beautiful woman — even a kid would notice that. But she looked me right in the eye and said it was nice meeting me, also. It was easy to see she was sincere. She had a warm, glowing smile and sparkling eyes. I couldn't help smiling as I walked away. What a nice lady. It seemed all of Mr. Sinatra's friends were nice and he would rarely fail to introduce me whenever someone new came around."

55 Capra, Frank. *The Name Above the Title — An Autobiography*. New York: The MacMillan Company, 1971.

56 *New York Post,* April 26, 1959.

"Eddie Robinson, Ms. Parker, Carolyn and Mr. Sinatra were all wonderful to work with, and, like Mr. Sinatra, treated me as one of the guys. I never got to meet Keenan Wynn. I also loved working with Dub Taylor (we talked a lot, especially about duck hunting) and Ruby Dandridge (whose daughter, Dorothy, was working on the sound stage next door at the time with Sidney Poitier, who I met later). Mr. Sinatra also introduced me to Sammy Davis Jr., who was great fun to be around. Sammy and Mr. Sinatra were close friends and showed great respect for one another. I was indeed blessed that my first experience making a movie was with the cast and crew of *A Hole in the Head*. There was never a moment of distress throughout the filming. Everyone treated me with dignity and respect, and I returned that with deep gratitude. There were so many fun times on and off the set. The only time I ever saw the cast again was at the Hollywood Premiere. I had not been allowed to see the rushes (dailies), so it was my first time to see anything we filmed. I was blown away at how all that work somehow became a movie."[57] Like Eddie, Joi was also happy with her appearance in the movie. "I had to act in the picture. I don't have a kissing scene. I was just like a flounder out of water."[58]

Frank Sinatra respected Joi for her acting ability and poise, and soon fell for the charms of his co-star. During the shooting of *A Hole in the Head*, he got romantically involved with Joi. Mike Connolly mentioned the affair with one sentence in his column. "Joi Lansing lit out for Las Vegas — because Las Vegas is where Frank Sinatra IS!"[59] In February, Columnist Earl Wilson reported that the fire between Frank and Joi had dimmed, "Shapely Joi Lansing's been going out stag since Lady Beatty [Shirley MacLaine] hit the West Coast and picked up her Frank Sinatra option," but he wrote in May that Joi's often seen on dates with Frank. An article called "Who's the Blonde Sinatra flipped for?" was published in *Tab* magazine. It states that Frank laid his eyes on Joi around 1956, but she chose not to become one of his regular girls. Their affair seemed more serious and based on respect. The article ends, "And how much of her time does Sinatra get? Joi isn't talking, but with Frankie usually away on location it's obvious she doesn't hit the night spot circuits with him often. She likes the coziness and solitude of her small apartment in Beverly Hills instead." Under the pressure of Frank's agency, the press reported that Frank and Joi were very close friends and that they intended to keep it that way.

57 Source: email contact with author.

58 *Utica NY Observer*, March 8, 1959.

59 January 27, 1959.

Singer Roberta Linn, the original Champagne Girl on the Lawrence Welk TV Show, performed in many of the Las Vegas hotels in the 1950s and 1960s. She became good friends with Frank and Dean Martin. "I worked Vegas for seventeen years. I met Joi there. At the time that I worked, when the Ratpack was there, Vegas was at its peak. We were like a family. We were all given long-term contracts. We did five weeks in January and would come back in March and do another five weeks. So we were all rotating and we became very close. Joi was a beautiful girl and I remember seeing her with Frank Sinatra. I saw her with him on different occasions. Frank was a real womanizer, he really loved pretty women. Joi was a beautiful, beautiful actress. She was just stunning and very sweet, very nice. She wasn't Hollywood nasty."[60]

Bill Corcoran, Joi's press agent in 1958 and 1959, explains why she was ambivalent about the affair. "Joi was very smart and very sweet. She was not a playgirl and I was surprised she started dating and even moved in with Frank Sinatra. She told me she couldn't stand Sinatra drinking all night, although she said he was wonderful to her and his best attribute was that he wanted to please any girl he was having sex with, and that included just about every starlet in Hollywood. I once attended a party before the Deb Star Ball with another client, Tuesday Weld, and all the young Hollywood starlets were bragging about the last time they had sex with Sinatra." Bill continues, "Over lunch one day, Joi told me she had to break up with Sinatra because it was impossible to handle all the calls he was getting every night from some of the biggest starlets in Hollywood who wanted to come to his house and spend the night with him. It was no secret in Hollywood, during the 1950s, that Frank Sinatra was a ladies' man. Gary Crosby, Bing Crosby's oldest son, once told me how he was staying at a hotel in Palm Springs and Frank Sinatra had rented an entire floor in the hotel and had brought from Hollywood some of the most beautiful starlets in show biz at the time to stay in the various rooms. Sinatra was a 'night person' and according to Gary he would spend the entire night going from one room to another to have sex with the various starlets. As the song goes, 'Nice Work if you Can Get it.'"[61]

Alexis Hunter remembers Joi telling her that she liked Frank a lot, but couldn't cope with his emotional and depressed moods. It was the main reason why she ended the affair.

---

60 Source: telephone conversation with author, 11-26-2017.

61 Source: email contact with author.

With Van Johnson and Frank Sinatra, 1958.

Frank Sinatra, Keenan Wynn and Joi taking directions from Frank Capra, 1958.

A Hole in the Head, with Frank Sinatra and Keenan Wynn, 1959.

Tiger Milk promotion.

Blonde Ambition

Joi starred in a succession of popular TV series in 1959. Besides her regular appearances on *The Bob Cummings Show*, she had parts in *The Jack Benny Program, The Lucy-Desi Comedy Hour* and *Richard Diamond, Private Detective*. In the latter, she was cast with Ruta Lee in an episode called "Jukebox." Ruta remembers Joi as a funny girl. "Joi Lansing was the one whose line I stole that I dearly loved. She was very amply bazoomed. Then she'd pad in a little more and I'd say, 'Joi, what the hell'…and she'd say, 'Please, I owe my whole career to B.F. Goodrich' [*laughs*]. Joi Lansing couldn't act her way out of anything, but she was a darling girl."[62]

In February, Joi was romantically linked to director, producer and actor Hugo Haas. Maybe through flirting with Haas she'd hoped he would star her in his productions as the successor of Cleo Moore.[63] He eventually chose former Miss Universe of 1957, Carol Morris to be his new leading lady in two of his movies. In April, the same gossip column makes mention that Joi's "real sweetheart is a lawyer, Paul Wolf."[64]

Joi attended trumpet player and band leader Ray Anthony's Capitol Records 10th Anniversary party on March 14. Two other blondes attended the party too: friend Sandra Giles and actress Jayne Mansfield, who came with her husband Mickey Hargitay. Judging from the photos that were taken that day, Ray only had eyes for Joi.

On March 24, she received the news from Ogden that her grandmother Grace had died in her sleep from a stroke. Joi left for Ogden immediately to be with her grandfather and family. On her return to Hollywood she had to put on a happy face when she and several other movie starlets were on hand as decoration for the opening of a Blum's candy store in Beverly Hills. A newspaper article covered the event and

---

62 Fitzgerald, Michael G. and Magers, Boyd. *Ladies of the Western*. Jefferson: McFarland & Company, Inc., Publishers, 2010.

63 *Albany NY Times Union*, February 13, 1959.

64 *Albany NY Knickerbocker News*, April 1959.

mentioned, "Among the outstanding guests we took down on the back of a menu, Miss Sandra Giles and Miss Joi Lansing. I have been queried on this by my teenage daughter. I find I did a rather disappointing job." The blondes didn't make an everlasting impression on the reporter, answering his teenage daughters question, "What did they look like?" with "They both looked like Jayne Mansfield."[65]

Joi joined the crew of *It Started with a Kiss*, who had returned from Spain to film the last interior scenes in Hollywood, in April. She has a couple of lines in a scene with Glenn Ford. A walk-on part in *But Not for Me* (1959) gave her the chance to work with Clark Gable again. In the picture his character is so distracted, that he — unlike all the other men at the swimming pool — doesn't notice her bathing suit clad beauty when she passes him by. Joi had been introduced to Clark Gable by glamour photographer Bernard of Hollywood, back in 1953. He recalled calling her and actress Barbara Nichols to have dinner with Clark and himself. "She didn't believe me. Clark in his Rhett Butler voice, 'Hello honey. We're starving, so get dressed and rush over.' Twenty minutes later, the two blonde glamour girls arrived dressed as if they were going to the governor's ball in *Gone with the Wind*. I introduced Joi and Barbara to Clark Gable. We ordered exotic dishes at Don the Beachcombers. Clark played it cool that night."[66]

Joi's contract for *The Bob Cummings Show* ended in the Spring of 1959. Apart from working on TV and doing films, she was thinking of new career directions to showcase the other qualities she possessed. Joi believed her physical appearance was still an asset to be recognized and to stay in demand. For five years she had been taking vitamin pills every day and kept a healthy diet combined with sports. It was Bob Cummings who had introduced Joi to the notorious 'Dr. Feelgood' in the late 1950s. Max Jacobson was an influential 'doctor' who used methamphetamines in a mixture of drugs. Robert received the so-called vitamin injections on a regular basis. Among Dr. Jacobson's clientele were Marilyn Monroe, John F. Kennedy, Frank Sinatra, Elvis Presley and Tony Curtis. Joi wasn't listed in his status of regular clients.[67] Paul Henning's wife, Ruth, recalls Bob's obsession with staying young. "Bob was a health nut, first and foremost. He took about fifty vitamin pills a day and shot himself in the fanny at lunch time with a special

---

65 *Desert Sun*, March 27, 1959.

66 Bernard, Susan. Bernard of Hollywood — The Ultimate Pin-up book. Cologne: Taschen, 2002.

67 Lertzman, Richard A. & Birnes, William J., *Dr. Feelgood*, New York: Skyhorse Publishing, 2013.

supplement. He exercised a lot, mostly swimming, but he was a good, all-round athlete and kept in extremely good shape."⁶⁸

Joi's next project, *The Atomic Submarine* (1959), started filming on June 18 and took eight days to complete. Brett Halsey was also in the movie. "On the movie *The Atomic Submarine* I met Joi and talked with her. I think she only worked one day. There wasn't time to socialize much. I was on

With Bernard of Hollywood.

the set when she was working. It was really kind of a fill-in scene. They had to have some sexy girl in the movie, because the scene did nothing for the plot. My memory of Arthur Franz is not really good. I don't wanna say he wasn't nice, it was as though he didn't want to be in the picture. He kept to himself. We did the principal photography in six days. You must be so well prepared. It's a great school for young actors. Either you do it and do it well, or you don't work."⁶⁹

---

68 Henning, Ruth. *The First Beverly Hillbilly — The Untold Story of the Creator of Rural TV Comedy.* Kansas City: Woodneath Press, 2017.

69 Source: telephone conversation with author, 07-01-2018.

Orville H. Hampton's screenplay described the scene. "Julie perched on the arm of an overstuffed chair, in all her lush female magnificence — contoured and accoutered elegantly — with fine legs, long and sexy. Julie is drool-bait." "That's the description Joi read in her copy of the revised shooting script dated May 26. That was the literary foundation on which she was to build her character. It can't have been that different from the description of every other part in every other picture she worked in or auditioned for. Almost two decades of finding yourself playing characters whose breast size is noted in the text."[70] Producer Alex Gordon recalled, "Joi Lansing was someone [Joe] Rivkin[71] proposed, and I gave way to him. I was told she was Frank Sinatra's girlfriend — or one of many [*laughs*] — and she'd work one day for 250 bucks. They probably wanted to use her in order to keep in good with Sinatra and especially the William Morris Agency, who represented her. I said, 'That's fine,' even though 250 bucks was a lot of money for us — we would have ordinarily paid a hundred bucks for that role. She turned out to be a very sweet girl, didn't bother us at all, had no airs."[72]

Whatever the nature of her friendship with Frank Sinatra, in June 1959 the press started spotting Joi on the town with Stan Todd, a Los Angeles investment broker. A couple of weeks earlier she'd met him at the home of a mutual friend. "It was a very romantic evening. Just like the song, 'Some Enchanted Evening.' I looked across the crowded room and I saw him and said, 'That's for me.' He didn't know it, but I had my eyes on him. Three days later he called me and asked me for a dinner date. From then on it was a whirlwind courtship."[73] Joi fell for Stan's charms and his shy nature. After dating for a couple of weeks, he still hadn't made a pass for her — of which she was both charmed and concerned. At the same time, it comforted her, because the men she had known before were only interested in one thing. Stan, ten years her senior, soon became her business manager.

Because of Joi's professionalism, Lucille Ball liked her a lot. She set up a meeting with Joi and told her that she wanted to put her under personal contract, to be one of her stock players. The 'Desilu Workshop'

---

70 Dougherty, Joseph. *Comfort and Joi*. New York: iUniverse, Inc., 2005.

71 Joe Rivkin was a casting director at Allied Artists at the time. "Although he had a good reputation in the trade, he was one of those rough, tough-talking people (with the bad language and everything) who worked for several studios."

72 Weaver, Tom. *Eye on Science Fiction*. Jefferson: McFarland & Company, Inc., Publishers, 2003.

73 *The Ogden Standard-Examiner*, June 3, 1962.

stock company consisted of less than two dozen performers who would be considered for casting in the many Desilu productions scheduled. Stan advised Joi not to do it, because he was afraid Lucille wouldn't let her do other projects. He hoped his wife would become a big star under his guidance. Joi trusted his opinion. The deal fell through, but Lucille and Joi remained friends throughout Joi's life.[74]

On August 22, Joi was invited to the farewell party of the famous Garden of Allah hotel at 8152 Sunset Boulevard.[75] Among the guests were her friends Dean Martin and Sammy Davis Jr. Most of the guests were dressed in 1920s fashion, booze flowed, former owner Alla Nazimova's surviving films were projected onto walls and people fell into the pool, a Garden of Allah tradition since 1929. According to Sheilah Graham's book about that event, someone also tried to push Joi in the pool that night.

The next month she flew to Salt Lake City to take part in a motor parade down Main Street in the afternoon. Together with Hollywood stars Barry Sullivan, Yvonne DeCarlo, Frank McGrath, Clu Gulager and Terry Wilson, she also appeared in a live version of TV show *Truth and Consequences*, emceed by Robert Barker. All activities were held on September 23, to boost the 1960 United Fund drive.

Due to her friendship with Dean Martin, Joi was cast in his new movie. She'd been mentioned in connection with *Who Was That Lady?* as early as August, but in November the press stated that a six-week search for two blondes described as 'sexpot entertainers' ended with the selection of Barbara Nichols and Joi. Additional scenes for the movie were filmed in late 1959. That makes the scene Joi appears in one of the last ones shot. The largest part of the production had been filmed between July 20 and August 25. In the film, showbiz sisters Barbara and Joi have a date with Tony Curtis and Dean Martin. What follows is a hilarious scene where the ambitious Coogle sisters think they are talking to CBS executives who can help them get a part on a show. The *New York Times* mentioned the two actresses in its review. "It gets even funnier when, with Miss Leigh braced for sacrifices 'in

---

74 Lucille divorced Desi and married Gary Morton in 1961. In 1967, the press mentioned that the Morton's gave a dinner party for Joi at Stefanino's. Some sources claim that Joi was Ball's regular stand-in on her TV show *The Lucy Show* (1962-1968). www.papermoonloveslucy.tumblr.com

75 Silent actress Alla Nazimova bought the property in 1918 and converted it to a hotel, which opened in 1927 as 'The Gardan of Alla'. The 'h' was added in 1930 by its new owners. The new owner, Bart Lytton — president of Lytton Savings and Loan — threw the farewell party; in October the hotel had been demolished to make place for his bank's main branch.

line of F.B.I. duty,' Mr. Martin drags her nervous spouse out on a double-date with two palpitating showgirls, Barbara Nichols and Joi Lansing." *The Motion Picture Herald* reports about the blondes' appearance, "Barbara Nichols and Joi Lansing play a typically narrow-minded but broadly-built pair of sisters [Dean] Martin is trying to seduce," and *Times-Union* summarized, "Dean Martin sings the title song, and Barbara Nichols and Joi Lansing, blonde sirens, help to complicate the complicated story."

Janet Leigh remembered in her autobiography, "We really rolled with this one. The personal familiarity of the three of us allowed absolute freedom, and the interplay was wild and woolly and inventive. There was an atmosphere of playfulness on the set that lent itself to practical jokes, attempts to make each other laugh in the middle of takes, and escalating water fights."

Assistant Professor of Chemistry at Columbia University, Tony Curtis, is caught in the act by his wife, Janet Leigh, while he is kissing a student. Because of the incident, she wants a divorce. Dean Martin, a writer for TV shows, helps his buddy out by thinking out a scenario that makes the two men FBI agents. Tony detests the idea, to which Dean makes him believe that he truly is an FBI man, confessing one minute later that if he falls for his lies, his wife surely will believe their scheme. They arrange the needed props, and an FBI identification card for Tony is made. At first, Janet doesn't fall for Tony's story and threatens to throw him out. But when she sees the ID card she's baffled and begs for forgiveness. Because the card wasn't used for a TV program, the prop man notifies the FBI about the fraud. Agent Powell pays Janet a visit. He soon finds out what's going on. Meanwhile, Dean picks up Tony for an assignment. Much to Tony's disagreement. He's the wiser one, and he wants to stop the charade. But Dean makes it worse by the minute, dishing up a story about two foreign spies they have to unmask.

> DEAN: "I've got two sensational dames. They're a sister act. They won't separate. They'll separate when they've got enough liquor in them."
>
> TONY: "I'm happily married. I don't want any outside women."

After 54 minutes into the movie, Barbara and Joi make their entrance. And what an entrance! After adjusting their stockings, they are greeted by the doorman of Wong's restaurant.

"Get a load of how these girls are assembled," Dean tells Tony. The girls join the boys in their booth. Barbara wants to eat a cookie, but suddenly stops, exclaiming, "I have to be careful what I swallow today." Dean claims that Tony is vice president for CBS, "and that he uses girls," as Dean likes to add. The meeting with the girls becomes sort of an audition, to land a part in a TV show.

DEAN: "You do use girls, don't you?"

BARBARA: "He thought you might use us."

DEAN: "I couldn't put it better myself."

Joi continues the conversation, "We're very versatile. We sing and dance."
"Like rabbits," Dean adds.
To talk things over amongst themselves, the Coogle sisters go to the powder room. There they call their agent for advice and they're overheard by Janet, who rushed to the restaurant with FBI agent Powell, because she wants to bring Tony his gun, which he left at home. The sisters' agent tells them that Tony is a phony and that Dean always tricks girls this way. The sisters are furious and say to each other that they could kill the men. Janet wants to warn the boys and hurries back to the FBI man, to tell him what she heard. Things get out of hand and the press is notified about a shooting in a restaurant. The boys and the Coogle sisters flee outside and are caught by a street full of reporters and TV cameras. Tony passes out, Janet comes to his relief. The scene with Joi and Barbara ends here, having lasted fifteen minutes.

When the FBI evaluates the disastrous event, their chief mentions that the two Coogle sisters have had no suspicion of their involvement. They were made to think that not they, but two other women were the foreign agents mentioned by the press. "They were taken home and put to bed." His secretary can't take that down, so he changes his sentence, "...were permitted to go to sleep."

Who Was That Lady? reached number nineteen at the box office for 1960. It grossed over $3 million. It was actress Dyanne Thorne's first film. "At the time, I was taking classes at New York University and was looking to make my mark and get started. I was working, as they call it, as an extra. I was working in a scene that was Janet Leigh's scene. Tony Curtis and Janet Leigh worked the day that I worked. I didn't get to meet Barbara and Joi on that movie, but the rumors on the set were that both these ladies were very easy to work with and just everybody loved their personalities. Their colleagues thought the world of them."[76]

Columnist Mike Connolly wrote in October, "I ran into Joi Lansing, whose walk-with-a-wiggle in *Who Was That Lady* belongs in the higher realms of art, along with the Tiller Girls, Mme. Tussaud's Wax Museum and Disneyland. I asked the doll whither she was wiggling. 'Over to Paramount,' said she, 'to see Perlberg. He wants me to play the kookie broad in *The Rat Race*."[77] She didn't get the part. Somewhere between October 19 and December 15, Joi worked with Jerry Lewis on *Cinderfella* (1960). The metamorphosis sequence, in which the Fairy Godfather transforms Fella for his appearance at the ball was shot as a large production number featuring the song *I'm Going to the Ball*, according to Paramount studio records. Besides Joi, actresses Francesca Bellini, Barbara Luna, Frances McHale and Darlene Tompkins appeared in the number, but it was cut before the picture's final release in December 1960.[78]

Back in Hollywood from Salt Lake City, she got a call that Burt Lancaster wanted her for a part in his production of *Elmer Gantry* (1960). She was to come over to read for the part of Lulu Bains. A date was set for the two to meet, but when she arrived at the studio, it seemed Burt had called her over for other purposes. There was no script to read from and when she understood what was going on, she brushed Lancaster off. She was furious and left immediately. The part of Lulu was played by Shirley Jones. Joi's step-daughter, Leslie Todd, remarked on the subject of sexual harassment, "She told me some of her stories. She'd go to meet the people she was going to be in a film with and, if they invited her into their trailer and left the door open, it was a good meeting. But, if they shut the door and locked the door behind her, she might as well get up and leave because they didn't really want to talk to her. They just wanted sex."[79]

---

76 Source: telephone conversation with author, 3-20-2015.

77 *The Philadelphia Inquirer*, October 23, 1959.

78 Although actress Barbara Luna is mentioned taking part in the particular scene, she herself says she didn't take part in the filming of this movie. (Source: email contact with author).

79 *www.desertsun.com*

With Ray Anthony, March 14, 1959.

Joi with Clark Gable on the set of *But Not for Me*, 1959.

But Not for Me, 1959.

Cosmetologist Max Factor with Joi, Jayne Mansfield and Arlene Howell. April 1, 1959.

Who Was That Lady, with Tony Curtis, Barbara Nichols and Dean Martin, 1960.

In rehearsal for *The Jack Benny Program*, 1959.

Publicity photo with Barbara Nichols.

Joi at Idlewild Airport, 1959.

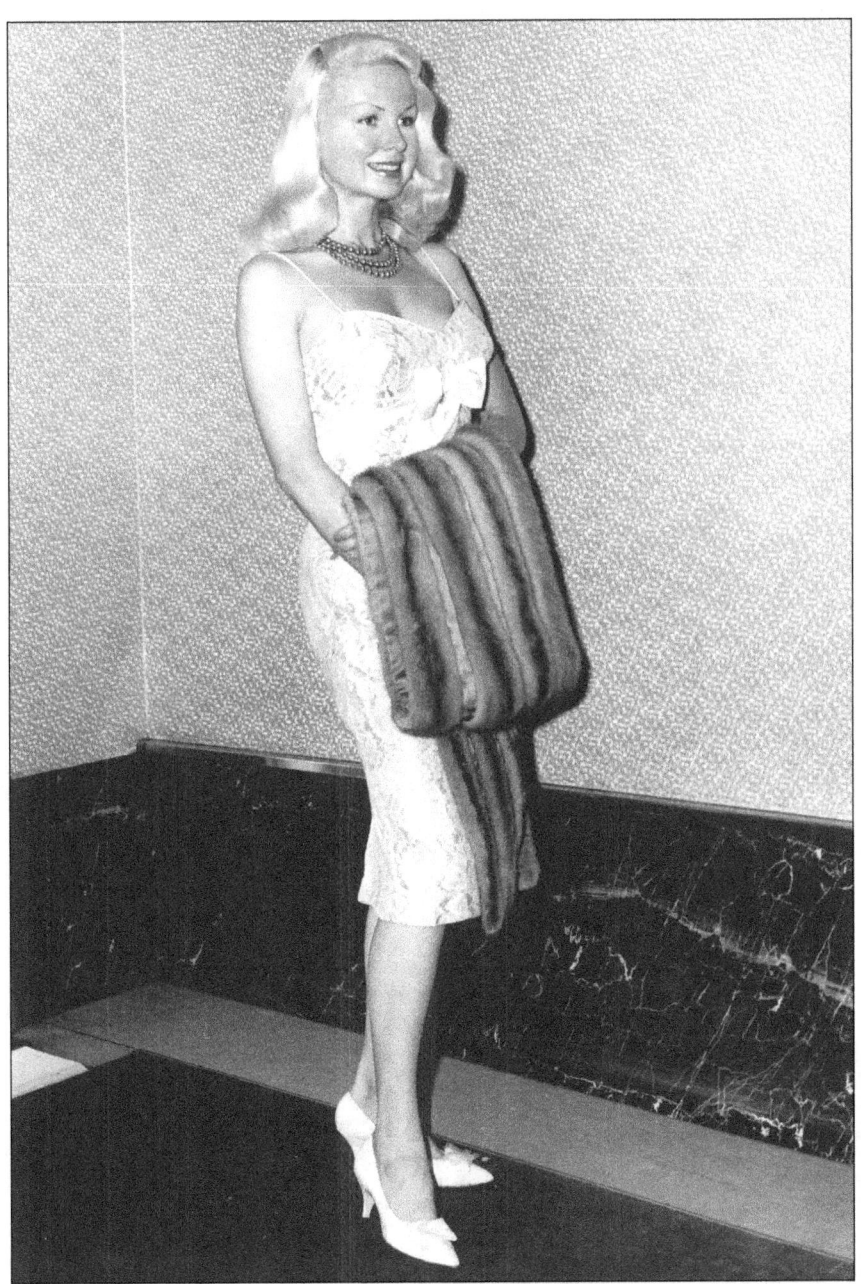

Arriving at the Criterion for the opening of *Who Was That Lady,* April 15, 1960.

Chapter 4: The Sixties

New Directions

The start of the new decade brought a lot of change, politically as well as economically. With the Cuba revolution still in mind, the already tense relationship with the Soviet Union grew to a new height in the early 1960s. A research report was published that one third of all Americans lived in poverty. In the South black students organized so-called sit-ins, peaceful demonstrations to address the wrong-doing they experienced every day. Demonstrations for civil rights and women's rights dictated the news. The approval of a birth control pill made the headlines in 1960.

In Hollywood, it was a rough time for actors, especially those without a studio contract. The major studios had made it almost impossible to build a career in the movies without their backing and support, but now the movie moguls and their old studio system were under attack. In March 1960, Screen Actors Guild went on strike against the seven major studios. This was the first industry-wide strike in the 50-year history of movie making. The Writers Guild of America had been on strike since January 31, 1960, with similar demands to the actors. The independents were not affected since they signed new contracts. The dispute rested on actors wanting to be paid 6% or 7% of the gross earnings of pictures made since 1948 and sold to television. Actors also wanted a pension and welfare fund. The actor's strike was led by SAG President Ronald Reagan and lasted six weeks.

On February 5, 1960, Joi received a star on the Walk of Fame.[1] It was a sign of recognition to be awarded with a star and it certainly gave her self-esteem a big boost. On the other hand, it was mere symbolism, and Joi was acute enough to know that a star on Hollywood Boulevard didn't bring her job security. Partly because acting jobs were scarce, Joi decided to focus on her singing talents. She commented later, "A few years ago, during the actor's strike in Hollywood, with the bills piling up and all, I took up singing."[2]

1 At 6529 Hollywood Blvd. Category: Television.

2 *TV Magazine*, August 1-7, 1965.

"You know what I want to do most?" she asked Hollywood reporter Joe Hyams during an interview. "I want to do musical comedy and sing and dance in Technicolor and Cinemascope."[3] She fulfilled one wish on her list when she cut a record album called *Joi to the World*. It's unclear if the album was ever released. Though not on her wish list, her marriage to Stan Todd was another positive event in her life. Alexis recalled that, "He was very important to Joi. She loved him very much. He was like the father she never had. She used to call him Grampy, the nickname she also used for her grandfather."[4] "I guess they fulfilled each other's desires, she being eye candy for him and he being daddy for her. He seemed to me to be an ok guy,"[5] Bill Marx mentions.

Joi shows her engagement ring with Stan Todd, June 3, 1960.

Stan had two daughters from a former marriage. Daughter Leslie had met Joi with her father several times in New York before the wedding. "At the Tuscany Hotel to be specific. But I did not attend the wedding. They lived in Los Angeles and I lived in Delaware."[6] Stan and Joi were engaged in June. Joi proudly showed her five-carat ring to the Hollywood' press boys. In August, the couple took out a marriage license in Los Angeles and they announced that the marriage would be on August fifth. During wedding preparations, Joi got the news that her father, Jack Glenn Brown, had died on June 18th.

The marriage took place at the home of their good friends Fred and Marjorie Mead, in Beverly Hills.[7] The ceremony was performed by

---

3 *Globe-Gazette TV News*, April 15, 1960.

4 Source: email contact with author.

5 Source: email contact with author.

6 Source: email contact with author.

7 Marjorie Mead, known as "Miss Dee," was head of *Confidential* magazine West Coast operations. Because of her job she was one of the most feared and hated persons in Hollywood.

Superior Judge Burnett Wolfson. After the wedding, the newlyweds left for a ten-day honeymoon on a friend's yacht to Mazatlan, off the coast of Mexico. After the honeymoon, they moved into their new home, a two-story contemporary, situated above the Sunset Strip in Hollywood. The house had an Olympic swimming pool on the second level, a fully equipped gymnasium, a steam room and a golf course. Joi was a strong swimmer, an avid tennis player and a trained horsewoman.

Joi and Pete Edgar. COURTESY OF PETE EDGAR

In the Summer of 1960, Pete Edgar was a young boy when he visited Joi at her luxurious home. "I was in *La Mirada Little League*. I played for the *Seals* and our manager was a man who knew people. I don't know what he did or anything, but Miss Lansing was not the only celebrity that I met when around him. As far as I can figure this was to be a publicity shoot, there was a photographer with us, for the Little League. I don't remember how many guys from the team went, but it was our manager and two coaches, one being my Dad. We went on a Saturday, I believe, and we went to where Dodger stadium was being built, so that was kind of cool. Later in the afternoon, we went to her house, which was somewhere in the hills of either Hollywood or Beverly. We got to her house and someone rang the doorbell and a voice said 'yes.' We were identified, and the voice said, 'come in.' Now, the fact she had an intercom really impressed us kids. When we got inside the voice said, 'please sit down and I'll be right down.' Now we were overly impressed. We kids sat by the fireplace and eventually she came down. She introduced herself to the coaches and then to us kids. She was very nice, and pretty, and made us feel really comfortable. We went to her patio and took some group shots and then some individuals. The individual shot I took with her I still have, by the way, was me being like the catcher and she batting. It was dark by the time we left, but another thing that impressed us kids was that her pool was further down the side of the hill that she lived on. We were really stoked by her house, nothing overly amazing just very cool. My memories of the event are of a very positive nature."[8]

In August, Joi started rehearsing for *Klondike*. She was very happy to be cast in a new TV series. Based during the gold rush of 1898 in Alaska, *Klondike* was filmed at Paramount Ranch in Augora, California. Joi belonged to the main cast and was featured in seven of the seventeen episodes of its one and only season. Ralph Taeger, James Coburn and Mari Blanchard were her co-stars. Joi was a favorite of many viewers. Her absence in the episode "Keys to Trouble" didn't stay unnoticed. "The Saga of Halliday and Durain continues unabated. This episode involves a stolen piano and a hijacked load of whisky. Wallace Ford is on hand to play an old drunk, and though he does a good job, he doesn't compensate for the absence of Joi Lansing. Bring back our girl!"[9]

Joi felt this new series gave her the chance to show her acting talents. "Up till now, I've been typed, but the *Klondike* people are giving me the opportunity to show dimensions other than the obvious ones."[10] "I've always been cast as a boudoir girl. Even Goldie in *Klondike* is a boudoir type, although she has more to do than look sexy."[11] Her tone in another interview was less glum. Asked if her sexy blonde image hindered her, she answered, "Why should it? It's kept me working. If a producer forgets my name, he has something to remember me by."[12]

---

8 Source: email contact with author.

9 *Oswego Palladium Times*, November 14, 1960.

10 *Daily Herald*, September 19, 1960.

11 *The Post Standard*, January 2, 1961.

12 October 16, 1960.

Renowned directors like Sam Peckinpah directed some of the episodes of *Klondike*, but nevertheless the show didn't catch on with the public. *Surfside Six* and *Hawaiian Eye* were both big hits over at ABC. So, NBC took the two male stars of *Klondike* and shifted them to a modern, sunny location. All of a sudden, *Klondike* was gone and *Acapulco*, starring Ralph Taeger and James Coburn, was there in its place. Mari Blanchard and Joi were not in the cast. Heavily advertised, with the heroes basking on the beach amid several bathing beauties, it couldn't miss...but it did...and the ratings were so much lower than those of *Klondike* that NBC threw in the towel after about eight weeks.

Concerning movie and television work, the years 1961 and 1962 turned out to be the least productive years in Joi's career. In February 1961, she was featured in nationwide papers in a photograph where she ties the laces of heavyweight boxer Bob Albright's gloves. Joi bought 25 per cent of the boxer's contract and declared that she was serious about becoming his manager. 'Big Bob' Albright, who had been inactive since 1959, planned to stage a comeback. Although considered a publicity stunt, Joi did receive her manager's license from the California State Athletic Commission. "At this point, there's no certainty that the CSAC will allow Joi in heavyweight Albright's corner when he fights. If they do, West Coast fans are in for an unexpected treat. Also, the TV show, *Klondike* is in for an unexpected plug. You see, Joi is the star of that show."[13]

Desilu announced that Joi was to appear in a pilot for a possible new TV series. Desi Arnaz had also contracted Tuesday Weld and Mamie Van Doren for the comedy called *Working Girls*. Joi was to be cast as Rosemary. With her pals Julie (Mamie) and Angela (Tuesday) she shares a Manhattan apartment from where we watch each of the girls' mishaps in trying to catch the perfect mate. It was to be produced for CBS. Mamie Van Doren remembers that she decided not to participate in it. With her stepping out of the project, Desilu decided to skip the entire show.

In April, Joi let the press know that she was working on a nightclub act. Besides arranging several appearances in night clubs on the West Coast and producing *The Joi Lansing Show* for television, Stan didn't manage to get any good work for her. Rumors about problems in their marriage started to hit the news. Columnist Lee Mortimer asked, "What's to the rumors of actress Joi Lansing and her new husband, Stan Todd? Not already!"

---

13 *Boxing Illustrated Wrestling News*, May 1961.

Publicity photo for *Klondike*.

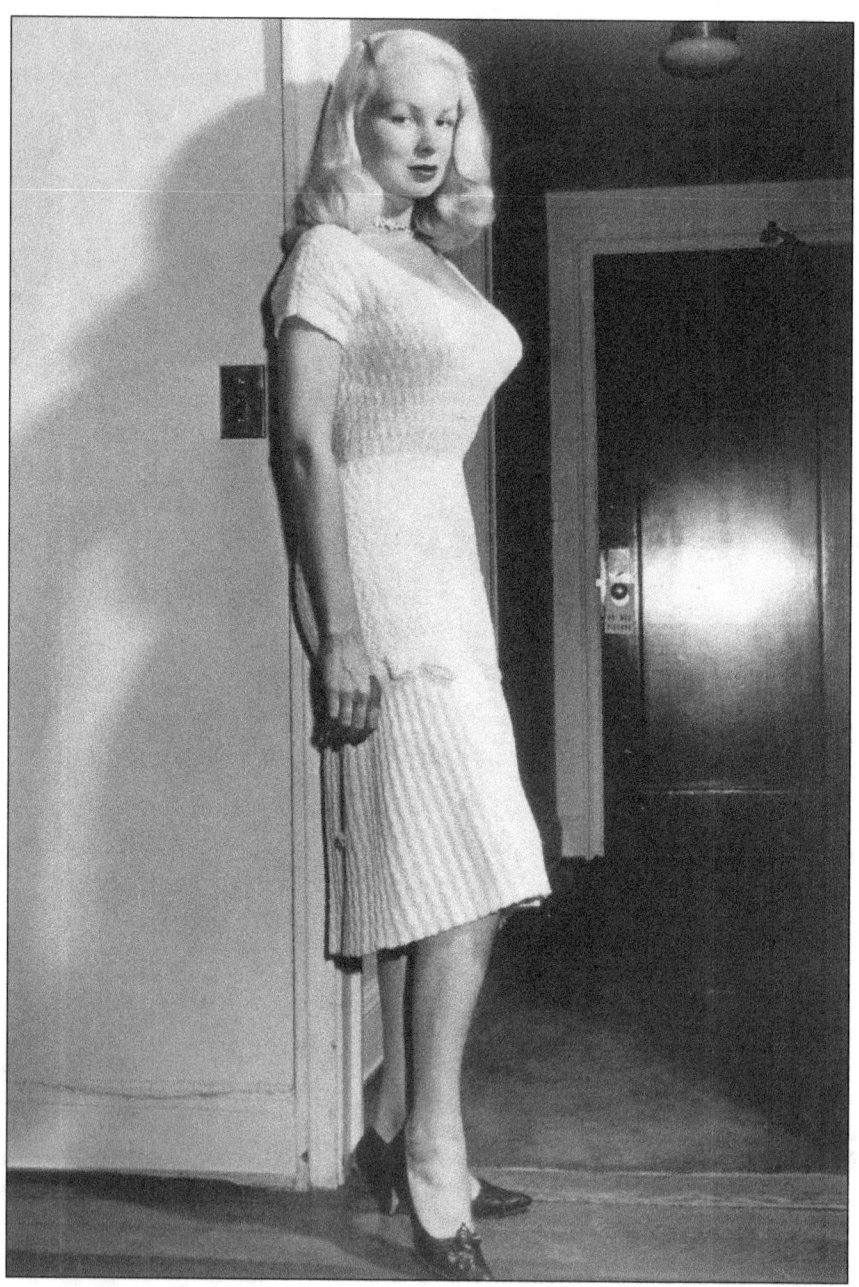

Candid photo.

Joi and Stan get their marriage licence, August 1, 1960.

The wedding day, August 5, 1960.

"WHEN A GIRL'S BEAUTIFUL"

With Bob Albright, 1961.

Joi consoles Bob Albright after his total knock-out defeat by Willie Richardson in San Jose, CA, March 1961.

Joi and Stan. COURTESY OF JOHN SHUPE

Joi performing in a night club.

The Singer, Not the Song

In January 1962, Joi signed a deal with Que Records to record a couple of songs and made her nightclub debut as a songstress at the Chi Chi Club in Palm Springs. The next month she was on her way aboard the SS Lurline to Hawaii for a singing tour. In Honolulu, she performed at the Royal Hawaiian Hotel. The tour took her to Sydney, Australia next. She entertained on the SS Lurline going over and on the SS Matsonia on her return to the United States. The first demo for Que Records was cut on February 23. Joi sang four songs. In April, she returned to the recording studio to cut several new songs. The recordings consisted of sultry lounge jazz numbers, with piano, drum and bass backing and songs with a Latin flavor. None of these test pressings were released on an album.[14]

On February 24, about 20,000 Division Soldiers and their family members were treated to a USO-type show called *Operation Reward*. The show was recognition for their sacrifice resulting from the mobilization as well as the hard work and training they devoted to achieving the STRAC designation. Twenty Hollywood stars, including Mort Sahl, Tom Ewell, Denise Darcel, Ann Richards, France Nuyen, Nick Adams, Frank Gorshin, Leslie Parrish and Joi, gave the Soldiers a three-hour show at Fort Lewis' Burris Field. The March edition of the Division's *Red Arrow* newsletter included a summary of *Operation Reward*. "The appearance here of a million dollars' worth of Hollywood entertainers for a performance for the 32d Infantry Division was a national news event. Numerous military and civilian dignitaries used the occasion as an opportunity to extend their greetings and best wishes. But it was the spirit behind these expressions which made them significant. The performers were not paid for the show; they came voluntarily despite tight personal schedules to thank us, in the most tangible way they knew, for our sacrifices in the cold war call up. They wanted to show us that our bloodless but forlorn battle here is recognized and appreciated."

---

14 The Que recordings of February featured the songs: "Masquerade is Over," "All of You," "The One I Love (Belongs to Somebody Else)" and "Who Cares." On the demo of April 30, "All of Me" and "Masquerade is Over" were cut again, with two new songs, "Feel So Young" and "Dream."

At this stage of her career, singing assignments and TV appearances were her main source of income. While visiting Ogden to share time with her grandfather at his birthday on May 28, she shared with the press, "I'm a chanteuse now, and I love it! This nightclub performing puts me into an entirely different world. I work all night and sleep all day, just the opposite from my picture and TV work."[15]

Nick Adams, Joi, France Nuyen, Tom Ewell and Maj. Gen. Herbert Smith, February 25, 1962.

Joi returned to Hollywood the day after to start shooting *The Joi Lansing Show*. The show was a platform to showcase her as a singer, dancer, actress in comedy skits and as the host interviewing her guest stars. The pilot never sold. Joi had hoped to develop into a dramatic actress, and she put her trust in the hands of Stan to manage her career in the desired direction. "My husband has plans for launching me into a dramatic role and is looking for a good script for me. I have always had to appear as sort of a dumb sex pot, but I'm really quite a 'ham' and would love to be starred in drama."[16]

15 *The Ogden Standard-Examiner*, June 3, 1962.

16 *The Ogden Standard-Examiner*, June 3, 1962.

In November, the press called Joi "a stick-out (in lots of ways)," at the celebration party for *How to Get Your Man and Hold Him*, another unsold TV pilot. On January 10, 1963, she took part in singer Eartha Kitt's fund raising for Synanon House, a non-profit rehabilitation center for narcotics addicts. She got a dance lesson from Eartha, who shared Joi's philosophy to stay sound in body and mind through physical exercise. All fees for the dance lessons went directly to the rehabilitation center. The next month, she made her debut in the first season of what was to become a very popular TV series, running for nine seasons.

The series followed the adventures of the Clampett family. After accidentally striking it rich, they move from their backwoods cabin to a Beverly Hills mansion, where their humorous hillbilly lifestyle clashes with their Beverly Hills neighbors'. *The Beverly Hillbillies* provided Joi with another iconic TV personality, Gladys Flatt, the glamorous wife of the real-life musician Lester Flatt.[17] Gladys dreams of becoming a movie star and a professional singer. "I play Mrs. Flatt and I'm getting to sing with the group. That's Paul Henning's [the producer] idea of a joke. He created the sex image for me on *The Bob Cummings Show*."[18]

The Beverly Hillbillies became a platform where Joi could display her singing talents, besides showing her gift in comedy acting, to a vast audience. The series drew nearly 60 million viewers a week in its peak years. Max Baer Jr., who played the family's son Jethro, recalled, "Joi knew Paul Henning, the creator of the show, because she'd worked on another of his series, *Love That Bob!* So, he put her in the series as Mrs. Flatt. Joi was a lot of fun. She was always laughing. She was a very, very nice person. She liked to joke and hear jokes, she was a great audience."[19]

Joi filmed a TV pilot called *Missy* for CBS. She played Missy MacDonald, a beautiful blonde who is dissatisfied with her work as a grocery clerk in a small town. She decides to leave for New York City, to seek new adventures. Playwright Garson Kanin wrote the one episode of this unsold TV show. When *Playboy* magazine approached her for a pictorial, she declined. Although Joi posed for titillating pin-up pictures during her career, she never took the nude-route like contemporaries Mamie Van Doren and Jayne Mansfield decided to follow in the 1960s.

17 Lester Raymond Flatt (1914-1979) is known for his membership in the Bluegrass duo The Foggy Mountain Boys, also known as 'Flatt and Scruggs.'

18 *The Sunday Press*, January 31, 1965.

19 Source: telephone conversation with author, 11-04-2017.

In May, Joi appeared in *Falcon Frolics '63*. The television broadcast honored the men stationed at the Vandenberg Air Force Base. In August the news of two policemen who were killed responding to a shooting at a bar shocked the country. Given her sensitivity to the agony and grief of other people, Joi took part in a fundraiser for the families of the slain Police Officers. Ronald E. Giles, who had seen Joi on television as a child,

Joi and Virginia, Christmas 1962. COURTESY OF JOHN SHUPE

found her to be much more beautiful in person when she visited his small hometown of Lodi, New Jersey in the fall. The year was rounded out with several nightclub performances and pre-production conferences with Stan about future film projects. She was mentioned in connection with TV's *Route 66* actor George Maharis, for a movie titled *I'll Build You a Town*, and the movie *Do it to a Stranger*, opposite Pat Boone, was discussed as a possible new project. Both productions failed to see the light of day.

Stan didn't manage to get her a movie part or much else work for that matter. His disability to manage her career was the main reason for many discussions and arguments between the two. When Joi found out she was pregnant, and Stan wanted her to have an abortion, she emotionally detached herself from him. Another low point in the marriage occurred when Stan dropped her off at the house of singer Les Paul, of the husband-and-wife duo Les Paul and Mary Ford, to have sex with him in exchange for a gig. Alexis Hunter thinks that Stan wasn't the right person to manage Joi's career. According to her he made major mistakes with her career and didn't treat her right. "Sex to Joi was just something you did. She wasn't particularly interested in it. Todd used her and sent her out on dates with producers, to have sex in exchange for a part in their productions."[20]

In November, a newspaper article mentioned that Les Paul considered Joi to replace Mary, whom he had recently divorced. But instead of working with Les Paul, she accepted the offer to replace actress/singer Abbe Lane and work with her ex-husband Xavier Cugat. "Cugie has spoken to me about signing on with him and I'm thrilled by the idea," Joi mentioned in an interview. She shared equal billing with Cugat during a stint at Hot Springs and was announced to tape a TV special with him in Lisbon, Portugal.

Christmas, 1962. COURTESY OF JOHN SHUPE

Actress Gloria Pall remembered a meeting with Joi and Stan, who were planning to sell their house. "In 1962, I opened a little lavender Real Estate office on the Sunset Strip. I became a broker after two years as a salesperson, catering to a celebrity clientele. Around 1963, I got a call from Joi Lansing to come to her house. She wanted to talk to me. She was married to a nice-looking man named Stan Todd and they lived in a modest little hillside house. We talked for a while and she wanted to show me something. We all got into my Mercedes and drove up a country road close by and we stopped at a little showplace type home in Laurel Canyon; a popular spot for artists, models, writers, and actors. The home had a huge pool and large decking around it. It was spacious and a very good floor plan and a perfect hideaway. 'Well, Gloria, what do you think we could get for this? We are thinking about selling it.' I told her a guestimate price

20 Source: Interview with author.

since it wasn't yet completed, and it would make a difference if it was turnkey ready. Joi said, 'Stan and I will talk it over and get back to you. Ok?' 'Ok,' I said, 'thanks for showing it to me and I know I can get you a good fair market price. Just call me when you are ready to list it and any way I can help you with any further questions.' I talked to her again and they weren't ready to list it and hadn't finished it. Several months later it still wasn't completed. I think they ran out of money, so it was at a standstill."[21]

In January 1964, Joi appeared at the Living Room Club. Her performance there marked her debut as a songstress in New York City. Old friend Mickey Rooney dropped in to see her show. Besides overwhelmingly positive reviews about her singing, her costumes also got mentioned frequently. She wore a black woolen evening dress that had the deepest décolleté allowed. The dress was held together with a black lace, leaving enough open to get a good glimpse of her amply bosom. "I had been taking singing and dancing lessons while I worked in TV, and about six months ago the opportunity arrived that I had been waiting for. I got a call from agent Ray Evans asking whether I'd like to come to New York and sing at the Living Room. Three weeks later I opened with tic wardrobe designed for me by William Naughton. In fact, the critics didn't review the act as much as they did the dress I wore. They called it the most talented gown in show business because of its décolleté."[22] Ray Evans' management gave Joi's career a huge boost. He arranged her lots of work, scheduling performances at established night clubs. Joi fell in love, and started an affair with him, which made Stan extremely jealous.

Joi attended the World Fair of 1964 in New York, held in Flushing Meadows, Queens, in April. She was crowned 'Queen of Candy' and reigned over numerous special events at the candy exhibit. She commented, "Candy, to me, is just like meat and potatoes to an athlete." Which was nonsense of course, because she was known as a health nut who didn't smoke, rarely drank alcohol, practiced several sports and was into yoga. She'd used Tiger Milk's nutrition bars and protein drink mix for more than five years. The company asked her to endorse their product and for publicity material, so Joi posed for photographer Peter Basch with a toy tiger and a box of Tiger's Milk.

Joi continued her night club act at the Glen Park Casino in Williamsville, N.Y. in May. At the time, it was speculated she had undergone an operation to enlarge her breasts. Alexis explained, "During the late '60s, silicone

---

21 Source: email contact with author.

22 *Times-News*, August 8, 1964.

implants were just starting to become an alternative to push up bras. It was a surgical procedure and pretty expensive for the average woman seeking larger breasts. The alternative was liquid silicone. Joi told me she'd done it because of the sex symbol image she portrayed. She knew a lot of people in L.A. who did it to get rid of wrinkles in their faces — even her friend, Frank Sinatra, had some injections by the doctor who had done her breasts and filled in her derriere. The shots achieved the look she wanted, since

Publicity photo, 1964.

her persona and image were all about her curvaceous body and firm, eye-popping cleavage. This was how she saw herself and how others wanted to see her. Ultimately, it became who she was. She was the sex goddess with the 'magnificent body' and she wouldn't let the years take this away."[23]

Joi was approached by producer Sam Spiegel, who considered her for a part in his motion picture *The Chase* (1966). By the time they started shooting, Joi had other obligations and Angie Dickinson was signed. On June 19, Frank Sinatra, Natalie Wood, actress Arlene Dahl and Joi were among the celebrities at the Motion Picture Relief Fund benefit. The MPRF was a service organization that offered health care and other services to entertainment industry employees and retirees. At the end of the evening the MPRF was $75,000 richer because of the generous gifts that were donated.

Singing was the main focus in her career and she performed regularly in nightclubs across the country. *Billboard* magazine reviewed one of her vocal performances. "Décolletage was defined with a capitol 'D' by Joi Lansing during her opening (no pun intended) at Gene Autry's Sahara Inn last week. The 39-23-35 thrush comes on stage singing 'I'm Just a Little Girl,' possibly the greatest understatement heard in a long time."[24]

A tragic event occurred when Joi's beloved grandfather passed away. He died on September 7, in Santa Clara, California, while he was visiting relatives. Joi was devastated with the loss of the man who'd supported and loved her all her life. Her life had no purpose anymore, and she fell into a depression. John Shupe recalls an event that cast an even darker shadow over Joi's grief. "When Grandpa Ray died, Virginia (I was told by my mother) had accused my father of not distributing all of the inheritance to family members. My dad was an honest man and I'm sure each person received every penny due to them. Virginia, I was told, convinced Joi and Larry that they as well as herself were cheated out of money and due to what Virginia said over many months they all decided they planned on suing my father. That broke his heart since he had done so much over many years to help them out financially and showing so much love and moral support to them all. No one followed through with their threats of taking him to court, but many hurt feelings remained. My mother was so offended that from that time on she wouldn't unwrap any gifts from Virginia and stored everything she received from Virginia in a closet."[25]

23 Hunter, Alexis. *Joi Lansing — A Body to Die For. A Love Story*. Albany: Bear Manor Media, 2015.

24 August 8, 1964.

25 Source: email contact with author.

With the help of alcohol and pills, Joi managed to work herself through her scheduled assignments. She hid her grief from her audience and received rave reviews for her shows. Joi's repertoire of songs included slow and sensual ballads, lively pop tunes, and a clever satire on Hollywood bombshells. One of her performances, at Chicago's Sahara Inn, was covered by reporter Milt Gentry. "Joi saunters up to the mike

Joi with unknown man after a nightclub performance, 1964.

in the most daring gown in all of legitimate show business. The bottom half of her dress clings to her slender gams like wet tissue paper, and the top half — well there almost is no top half. It roughly approximates two wide shoulder straps joined somewhere in the neighborhood of her navel, and it is filled to overflowing with a figure that makes Jayne Mansfield look like Fred Astaire. So it is no wonder that Joi can open the eyes of the deadliest audiences; but — like her necklines — she does not stop halfway. Joi also knows how to sing in a voice as silky as her platinum hair. Her tone, timing, and diction has a professional polish that almost make her sex appeal superfluous."[26] Milt spoke with Joi after her performance.

26 *Modern Man* magazine, November 1964.

He asked her about the difference between acting and singing, to which she replied, "It's the most stimulating thing in the world to work in front of a live audience after spending so much time in television and movies. The camera can be quite cold, but when the audience is with you — well, you can just feel the vibrations. There is nothing like it."[27]

In November, the papers mentioned that comedian and close friend George Jessel had plans to take a show to Korea for Christmas and New Year's to entertain the troops. He was planning to take Diane Findley, Jayne Mansfield and Joi. "The boys can listen to me and look at the girls," Jessel said. A couple of nights earlier he and the girls had run through their routines at a special performance at the motion picture country home. There are no records if the show and Joi made it to Korea. Stan announced in December that his wife would be starring in a new film with George Hamilton and Geraldine Chaplin. *Project 22* was planned to start filming in February 1965, in Egypt and Yugoslavia. The project never materialized. Instead of working on new film projects, she signed a contract, for a four-week engagement, to sing at the Queen Elizabeth Hotel in Montreal, Canada.

Because of her touring the countries' nightclubs most of the year, the rumors that the Lansing-Todd marriage was beginning to show cracks once again intensified. An unmentioned reason for the marital problems was the affair of Joi and Ray Evans. All her nightclub work was arranged by Ray. He also secured her a part of Dean Martin's sexy secretary in Frank Sinatra's upcoming movie. This angered Stan, and although they had an agreement to live together as friends, he wanted to be the only man she would depend on. Stan and Joi decided to separate. In December, Joi left for New York to be with Ray. In "the Big Apple" she attended a workshop session led by teacher Lee Strasberg at the Actors Studio. "Joi Lansing, who has been known primarily as a comedienne — with a fabulous figure in her show business career so far, has her mind on more serious progress. She's studying singing with vocal coach Carlo Menotti and learning to act via the Lee Strasberg method."[28]

She appeared as the 'Queen of Hearts' at the second Annual Ice Harness Races and Winter Sports Carnival, at White Lake, New York, in February 1965. A press release stated that she returned to Manhattan to record an album for RCA-Victor. The album had a couple of songs that were especially written for her by composer Jimmy Haskell and actress

---

27 *Modern Man* magazine, November 1964.

28 *Jamestown (N.Y.) Post Journal*, December 11, 1964.

Stella Stevens. "Talk about surprises," Joi mentioned, "Most actresses usually fight you in this town, but Stella heard me sing and called me up to tell me that she was writing some songs especially for me. Her lyrics are just beautiful." [29] *The New Yorker* mentioned in its 'Talk of the Town' column that Joi, Jan Sterling and Art Lund would become the disc jockeys for a proposed WCAB radio program that was to be broadcasted exclusively to cabdrivers and their passengers. Joi taped a pilot program, but the actual show never reached the New York City cabs.

In March, she sang at the Shoreham hotel in Washington D.C. One Washington critic admitted that he, "…was completely taken by surprise, Miss Lansing can sing." While another Washington critic, John Segraves, mentioned that, "This is not because Miss Lansing (39-23-35) has any of her songstress rivals shaking in their shoes. She is not going to make you forget Judy Garland, Barbra Streisand, Peggy Lee or anyone else who strikes your fancy." He continued, "When she saunters onto the Blue Room stage clad in a clinging, floor-length black gown with a neck line cut down to here, one gets the immediate idea that if she could perform, she wouldn't be trying to out Mansfield. However, her show was not one of extreme disappointment; in fact, most first-nighters got more than they expected — talentwise, that is. Joi's up-tempo tunes, such as 'You're Nobody till Somebody Loves You,' her own version of 'Hello, Dolly!' and 'It All Depends on You,' were handled in a free and easy voice; husky but capable. However, this is not yet a girl who can do much with a ballad. Things such as 'As Long as He Needs Me' and 'Call Me Irresponsible' were done in a rather awkward, caution-filled manner. She gave the impression she was walking down a spiral staircase in the black of night hoping not to miss the next step. The rest of her act, except for one two-minute sequence where she tried to be funny and wasn't, consists of walking around ringside making men blush while singing 'Teach Me Tonight' (she almost sat in one man's lap; he probably won't have those slacks pressed for months) and otherwise allowing everyone who cared to gaze upon her, well, gaze while she sang. Joi is something of a rarity for a room which caters to a great degree to anniversary and birthday parties and to such performers as Nelson Eddy, Enzo Stuarti and Robert Goulet. The impression here is that Miss Lansing would not be nearly as eye-popping if seen in the Latin Quarter or the Copacabana in New York City. A swank supper club seems somewhat the wrong place for this Lady Bountiful, at least until she reaches the point where

---

29 *Corpus Christi Times*, April 19, 1965.

her talent will allow her to tuck herself in a bit more. But it must be said she probably sent every male home to greet his wife with something like 'Hello, Harry.'"[30]

In May, Joi performed at Bimbo's 365 Club in San Francisco. On June 19, she was a vocalist at the benefit show of the Coin Machine Division at the Statler-Hilton Victory Dinner in New York and in August, Joi was scheduled to appear at the Cal-Neva lodge at Lake Tahoe, California. Joi's singing career really took off in the mid-1960s. To appeal to the young crowd and to keep an aura of youth around her, she claimed she was ten years younger than her actual age of 36. According to Alexis Hunter, Joi always lied about her age. "Joi didn't want anyone to know her actual age, so she deducted ten years. That way she could easily remember the age and birth date she had told everyone."[31] *Time* magazine saw through her deceit. "A year ago, she was a sexy, professional dumb blonde of 36 who posed for photographers doing dumbbell exercises to improve her 39-in. chest and promote the grade B flickers she appeared in. Now Joi Lansing is a sexy, smart, successful nightclub singer of 27 who has just finished making her first record. Her new press agent may be watching the wrong figure, or else Joi was only twelve when she got married in Juarez, Mexico, 15 years ago."[32]

Close friend Sandra Giles arranged a party for Joi to celebrate her success as a singer. There was a near-fight among some of the guests that disrupted the celebration. Photographer Arnie Sugarman accused Ray Anthony of trying to steal his girl, starlet Gunilla Hutton. He was going to clobber Ray, but Ray Evans talked him out of it. "If Anthony ever does it again," threatened Arnie, "I'm going to step on him!"[33]

While playing the nightclubs, Joi took the time to see the shows of other performers that were in town. Joi asked friend Ken Mayer to accompany her to one of Trini Lopez's performances when she worked on the East Coast in June. "At that time, Lopez was appearing in Blinstrub's Village and, he being one of her favorites, she asked me if I would take her to catch his show the following evening. I not only obliged, but for three successive nights we sat ringside at Trini's performances, and when the shows were over, Joi sat with his other invited fans in the privacy of his dressing room. And they'd sit there until the club closed, and on each

30 *The Evening Star*, March 4, 1965.

31 Source: email contact with author.

32 *Time magazine*, April 30, 1965.

33 *New York & Brooklyn Daily*, May 30, 1965.

night, we'd end up in Ken's at Copley for a late coffee and snack. Lopez was both flattered and amazed at the interest shown his act by Joi and together they'd make showbiz talk until even the help left. When finally the 'party' broke up, we'd drive her to the Ritz, say our good nights, and arrange to meet the following night. As much as she enjoyed talking to Trini, he seemed to enjoy it more, and there followed from that chance Boston get-together, a friendship that endured until her death."[34] Trini recalls, "In Boston, she came to see my show one night. I was very surprised. The Blinstrub's was the most popular night club in Boston. And after I did my hour show, she came over to my dressing room. And then I had to do another show, one at eight, the other at twelve o'clock. I don't remember if Joi visited that show too, but probably we did get together the other day in Boston."[35]

34 The *Boston Herald,* Aug. 15, 1972. Ken Mayer held a full-time job issuing press credentials for the Boston Police, and acted as a press spokesman for the Boston Police Commissioners Office. He also pounded out entertainment columns ("Night Mayer") for the Boston Herald-Traveler and later the Herald, and was one of the few Herald staffers that stuck when the Boston Record-American took over.

35 telephone interview with author, 06-01-2017.

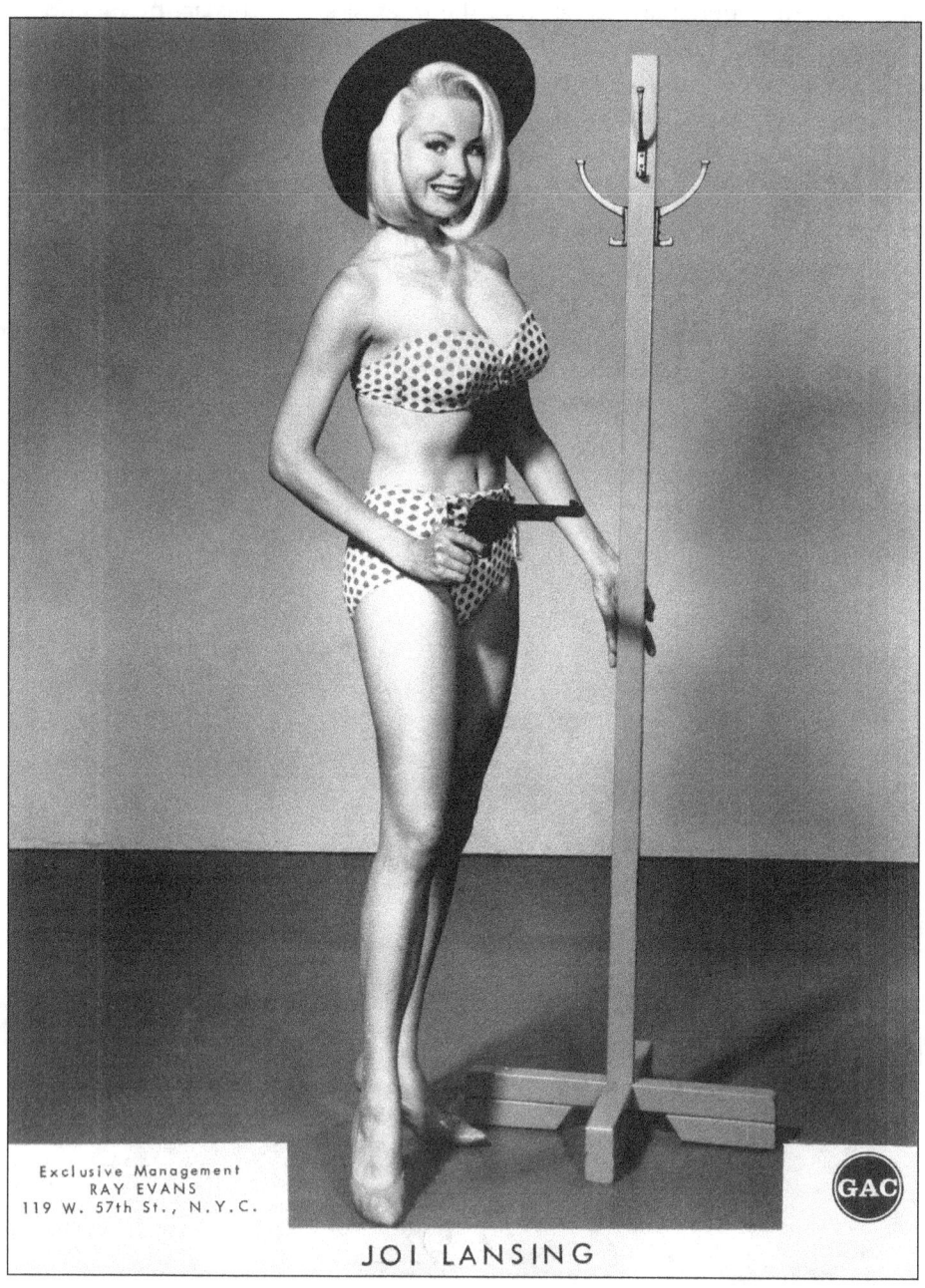

Agency photo, 1963.

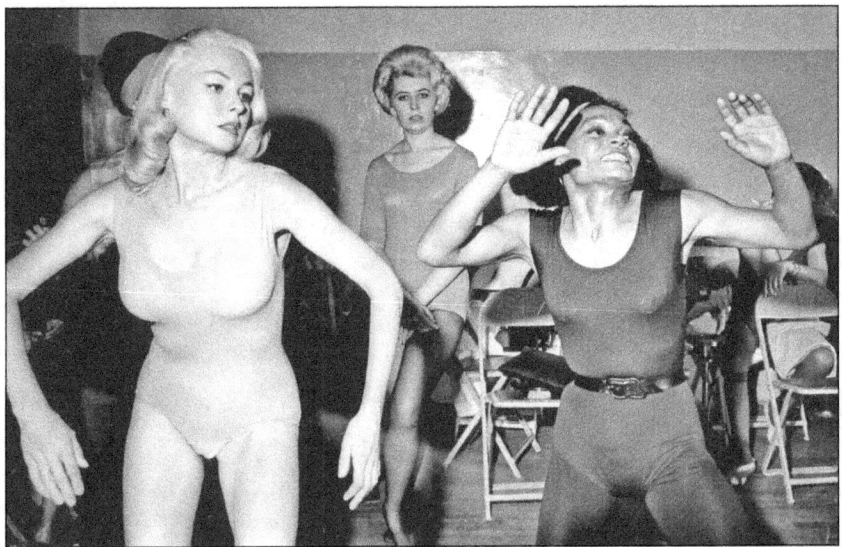
Ballet class with Eartha Kitt, January 10, 1963.

Joi at the Worlds Fair in New York, April 1964.

The Joey Bishop Show, 1963.

Publicity photo, 1964.

Marriage on the Rocks

The prophetic title of her next movie was of course purely coincidental, but Joi was not the only one on the set of *Marriage on the Rocks* who'd experienced marital problems. Filming had commenced on March 8, and Joi was signed by Artamis Productions Inc. on July 27. She joined the cast in August, to film her scenes. Joi was back on a movie set after a hiatus of five years. "People who never noticed me before pay attention to me since I've taken up singing. When Frank Sinatra asked me to play Dean Martin's swingy secretary in *Marriage on the Rocks*, I said, 'Sure.' It was a real groovy part."[36] Joi played Lola. She walks around in tight-fitting dresses and in a tiny polka dot bikini. The latter was used in the publicity photos, with Joi in different poses, showcasing her magnificent physique. Her last scene in the movie is with Dean Martin and Frank Sinatra. "Joi stands there after Sinatra exits, winking at us and her old boss during a music cue unctuous with saxophones. A beat and Sinatra returns, taking Joi by the upper arm. A look to Dean and to us communicating 'Sorry, old pal, this is mine now,' and he whisks her out of the office."[37]

Dancer and actor Christopher Riordan recalled working with Joi, and the atmosphere on the set of *Marriage on the Rocks*. "We were both in a film called *Marriage on the Rocks*. However, we had no scenes together. Still, she was on the set a few times while I was working. And vice/versa. I had already worked with Sinatra prior to this picture (in *Von Ryan's Express*) so I was aware of how Frank behaved...on the set, off the set, and with the women he was interested in. In this case, this was a woman he *had* been interested in, but was still on friendly terms with. Joi was respected but kept at a distance. Perhaps because Frank's daughter, Nancy, was also in the picture; I don't know. I worked with Nancy again later, and we both discussed how our respective marriages were, indeed, 'on the rocks.' I was having problems at home, and to make matters worse, the girl I had been seeing before my marriage was also in the film. [Darlene Lucht who was

---

36 *TV Magazine*, August 1-7, 1965.

37 Dougherty, Joseph. *Comfort and Joi*. New York: iUniverse, Inc., 2005.

then known as Tara Ashton.] Nancy was about to shed Tommy Sands. *Rocks* was an odd set. Perhaps because of all the personal problems. But I noticed that none of this affected Miss Lansing. She went about her business in a most professional manner, and that seemed to please everyone."[38]

Trini Lopez was also cast. His performance was filmed in one day. "My appearance on the movie was a cameo. It was a night club scene and I

Following acting classes at Lee Strassberg's, New York 1965.

sang one of my songs. There were a lot of nice, pretty ladies on that movie. We were all standing around, waiting for the lights to be set up. We had a really nice time. Everybody was so happy and cordial. It was a very happy set. I thought Joi was very sexy. Her persona was very, very sensual."[39]

While Joi was working on the West Coast in May, the press reported that Joi and Stan were seeing each other regularly, but in September and October, Joi thoroughly enjoyed the company of Ray Evans, while Stan was seen around town with starlets Marci Mann and Juli Reding. In the fall of 1965, Joi had singing engagements at the Copacabana nightclub, the Waldorf-Astoria and the Americana Hotel in New York City. She

---

38 Source: email contact with author.

39 Source: telephone interview with author, 06-01-2017.

entertained the audience with several jokes delivered in a self-mocking style that emphasized her dumb blonde image. "I live there, and I can tell you that to succeed in Hollywood you simply must have a gimmick. Leslie Caron talks with her big eyes, Jimmy Durante talks with his big nose. Jayne Mansfield and I are pretty talkative, too." And "Who says I'm not smart? Last week a salesman told me he had a vacuum cleaner that would cut my housework in half. So I bought two of them." The review in the *New York Journal—American* called Joi a revelation. It read in part that Joi's "…one of the most improved performers we have encountered this season." She continued to tour the nightclubs, with bookings at the Fontainebleau in Miami and, from October 19 through October 23, at the Persian Terrace of the Hotel Syracuse in New York City.

Clarence Potter attended one of her shows. "I attended a midnight Joi Lansing show at the Diplomat Hotel in Hollywood, Florida in early February. Joi appeared in the hotel's Tack Room. We were very lucky to be seated at a table right next to the stage. Joi came out in a beautiful beige floor length tight gown. From the waist up the gown had a see-through beige netting and she was absolutely gorgeous. She was everything I could ask for including a wonderful singing voice. She stood next to me several times during the show. The stage was on the same level as the audience. Also appearing at the Diplomat in the much larger Café Crystal was Judy Garland. We were also seated next to the stage for Judy's show after giving the maître d' an enormous tip. Judy's show is another story, but it was awesome. It's kind of funny that we sat next to Judy's husband at both shows. Back to Joi. Joi did a great tribute to Frank Sinatra, singing several of his hits while wearing a black fedora hat. I forgot to mention that Joi also used a white fur as sort of a stage prop. She was fabulous! *Variety* gave her a great review. All in all it was one of the most exciting nights of my life!"[40]

A raving review read, "Watching Joi Lansing sing is a joy and the fact that she had laryngitis hardly made any difference at opening night at the Persian Terrace where she will appear through Saturday. It only resulted in a huskier, intimate nightclub voice which is quite her style. The glamorous actress of movies and television drew a full house Tuesday night at Hotel Syracuse. At 39-23-35, Joi's every inch the popular concept of what a starlet should be, and she satirized the image in a song about the 'Starlet who Won an Anatomy Award.' Her latest motion picture, *Marriage on the Rocks*, starring Frank Sinatra, is playing now at RKO Keith's and she told the audience about her playing Lola, personal secretary to Dean Martin,

---

40 Source: email contact with author.

in the comedy. Then she sizzled her way through 'Whatever Lola Wants, Lola Gets.' In honor of Sinatra, she donned a hat and slung a trench coat over her shoulder to sing a medley of his songs. Joi made a striking fashion entrance in a black evening gown, with a chiffon top. The high neckline was slit in the back to the waist while the figure-hugging skirt was slit to the knees — in order to let her move."[41]

On January 20, 1966, Joi visited the city of Lansing, Michigan. Senator S. Don Potter made her an honorary citizen and the Lansing Fire Department elected her as their honorary fireman. When asked why she decided to take Lansing as her stage name, she admitted that she had picked the name Lansing out of the blue.

Stan and Joi reconciled and moved into their new home in Woodland Hills, in the southwestern area of the San Fernando Valley. The couple shared with the press that the main reason for their breakup was Joi's continual absence while being on tour. When Sandra Giles threw her a birthday soiree, Joi attended the party with Stan. Sandra's daughter, singer Sandra Piller, remembers meeting Joi. "I do remember her. I was a very little girl, but I do remember she was always happy and very nice."[42]

In 1966, Joi became one of the faces and voices for Scopitone, a jukebox with video clips. Irving Briskin, the executive producer of Harman-EE Productions who produced the music films for Scopitone, signed singer January Jones and Joi to an exclusive five-year coin machine contract in April. Among the other recording artists that were contracted were Debbie Reynolds, Kay Starr, Vic Damone, Della Reese and Frankie Avalon. Joi's songs are titled "The Silencer," "Web of Love" and "The One I Love Belongs to Somebody Else," which she performed in various stages of undress. She was looking more voluptuous than ever before. In "Web of Love," she's caught in a giant spider web, boiled in a witch doctor's cauldron, and chased by snakes. In mid-1966, Joi had filmed a music clip for the Color-Sonics film jukebox at Paramount Studios in Hollywood. It's titled "All of Me," and is lesser known than her Scopitone song clips. Joi hoped that she could combine singing and acting for a living. "I've been studying dramatics and my singing is helping me to develop as an actress. From now on, I intend to project an image of an actress who sings, not a sex symbol."[43]

Singing engagements took Joi on the road again. U.S. Marine Mike Marx attended one of her shows in the spring. "It was during my time

---

41 *The Post Standard, Syracuse, N.Y.*, October 21, 1965.

42 Source: email contact with author.

43 *TV Magazine*, August 1-7, 1965.

on active duty with the U.S. Navy that I had the distinct pleasure of meeting one of the most beautiful and stunning actresses/singers of her time, Joi Lansing. I was stationed in Newport, R.I. aboard the USS Hammerberg (DE-1015) from February 1966 till December 1967. We had been in Boston being overhauled and had just got back to Newport when I found out about the show coming up in a few days. Miss

Joi with Mike Marx, May 1966. COURTESY OF MIKE MARX

Lansing came to entertain the troops for our Annual Cruiser-Destroyer Force, U.S. Atlantic Fleet Spring Ball in May. The evening consisted of a Buffet Dinner from 6-8 pm at 8 pm with Welcoming Remarks by Rear Admiral R.A. Ruckner and at 8:15 pm the show opened with the 'Kirby Stone Four' followed by the stunning Joi Lansing who whoad the crowd. She had platinum blonde hair, large blue eyes and a voluptuous figure. She wore a two-piece white outfit, the top was lace with white brocade with sequins covering the breast and a long, to the floor white matching skirt. Today, it reminds me of a Bob Mackie gown. She certainly had all of the men's attention as she sang her songs. I don't remember what she sang but they were in the Pop genre. She was a polished performer and put on an excellent show. I got to meet Joi after the show and she couldn't have been more pleasant. What a wonderful evening! I never thought of it at the time, but here was a lady whose competition was Marilyn Monroe, Jayne Mansfield and Mamie Van Doren. Not bad company!"[44]

On August 4, Joi and Red Buttons performed in the Fiesta Room in Las vegas, Nevada, for one month. Jayne Mansfield and Buddy Lester were booked for the next month. In Vegas, Joi met old friends Ruth and

Joi performing, May 1966. COURTESY OF MIKE MARX

Paul Henning. Ruth remembered, "Las Vegas brings to mind Joi Lansing, one of the gorgeous models who graced *The Bob Cummings Show* regularly. She was appearing there, and one day came over to visit and sun with us by the Desert Inn pool. We were lying there with our eyes closed, but it was no trick to guess when Joi made her entrance. There was a chorus of male 'Ahhhhhs.' Joi was blonde and beautiful, with long legs, narrow hips, and a very large bosom, thanks to plastic surgery. Even if I hadn't known about that, I would have guessed because when she lay down, her bust still stood straight up. Nature simply doesn't do that. Joi was a nice girl. The figure enhancement helped her to make a living, and nobody can be blamed for that."[45]

44 Source: email contact with author.

45 Henning, Ruth. *The First Beverly Hillbilly — The Untold Story of the Creator of Rural TV Comedy.* Kansas City: Woodneath Press, 2017.

Beside working as a singer, she was tested for a new TV series and was mentioned for a part in *The Silencers* (1966) with Dean Martin. The TV series was never made, and she lost the role in *The Silencers* to Stella Stevens. No other movie offers came her way. Joi complained about the invasion of European actresses that swarmed all over Hollywood. Even Frank Sinatra had chosen the talents of Austrian Senta Berger and Italian Virna Lisi to be his leading lady. "I would suggest that being born in Spoleto, Marseilles or Stockholm is not anything magical, accent or no accent. I would ask our producers to beat the bushes of Akron and Denver and Phoenix. If they'd stop ogling the ladies overseas, they might be surprised at what they found in their own backyard."[46]

Joi's contract with Scopitone demanded that she would be on hand for publicity conventions to promote the video-jukebox. On Friday, October 28, Joi attended the Music Operators of America convention. She took her job to publicize Scopitone seriously, meeting and taking photos with convention visitors the whole morning and afternoon. She said, "Everybody's been very nice, but I've been on my feet so much I feel like I'm going to die."[47] On Wednesday, November 3, a reception was held at the Tel-A-Sign offices on Madison Avenue in New York City, where the film-music machine was on display for local press and members of the trade. The reception was hosted by Pioneer Vending Company president Bill Steiger, Scopitone sales executive Jack Mitnick and Joi.

A Los Angeles mail-order company, the Howard Diamond Co., used her as their "come-on." Her pictures adorned their ads and they offered free pin-up photos. Since the company advertised in-service publications, there were thousands of requests and Joi became one of the favorite pin-ups of the Vietnam war. She treasured a letter from a sailor stationed in Vietnam, which included this excerpt, "I slept with your picture under my rock last night and dreamed about you all night." Joi supported the American service-men throughout her career.

On November 19, she appeared as 'The Queen Venus' of the annual Artists and Models Ball at the Hotel Biltmore, to celebrate the 90th anniversary of The Kit Kat Club, an artists' group celebrating the Arts, originally founded in England. Among the former Queens were Jayne Mansfield, Julie Newmar and Greta Thyssen. The ball was considered the most outstanding and spectacular annual costume ball in the United States. Joi's King Jupiter was actor Eddie Bracken. The festivities started

---

46 *Des Moines Sunday Register*, August 7, 1966.

47 *Cash Box*, November 12, 1966.

at 9:00 p.m. At 10:00, Their Majesties judged the costumes of all guests at the Throne Room and at 11:45 the King and Queen and their Royal Court Attendants made their entrance at the Grand Ballroom. They opened the ball, which went on until 2:00 a.m.

Joi headlined a show at the Caribe-Hilton in San Juan, Puerto Rico for two weeks in November. In the previous six months she had made café appearances across the country. "And everywhere I went, I found audiences eagerly waiting for music that is music." Joi predicted that the return of the big band would change the sound of the day. "The gimmicks the Beatle-type kids employ now are just that — gimmicks." Joi had always been conservative in her tastes in music and her choice in repertoire. "In recent months, we have seen the return of the twelve or fourteen-piece band in key spots. And these are not just the back waters of show business. They always have been considered avant garde — New York, Las Vegas, Chicago. From where I sit, the big band is not only going to bring back music but sanity!"[48]

When she returned to the United States, she signed a contract to do a movie for Woolner Brothers' production company and negotiated with producer Bob Lippert to appear in *Heart of Darkness*. The movie for Lippert was never made.

In Woolner Brothers' *Hillbillys in a Haunted House* (1967) she played the part of Boots Malone.[49] Filming started in December under the working title *Ghost Party*. The movie is a mix between a musical comedy and a spy thriller. Singers Ferlin Husky and Boots Malone are on their way to a Country Music Jamboree. When their car breaks down, they have to stay overnight in an old mansion. The place seems haunted but is actually the hide-out for some criminals. In late January, the picture was completed. *Hillbillys in a Haunted House* is dotted with several country music performances. Joi sang, "Part-Time Lover" and "Gowns, Gowns, Beautiful Gowns." Classic horror movie stars Basil Rathbone, John Carradine and Lon Chaney Jr. also took part in the production.[50] Lippert started pre-production for a third sequel, *Hillbillys in Outer Space*. He considered Joi for the female lead.[51]

---

48 *LA Herald Examiner*, November 1966.

49 Mamie Van Doren had played Boots Malone in *Las Vegas Hillbillys* (1965). She declined to appear in the sequel *Hillbillys in a Haunted House*.

50 "The making of *Hillbillys in a Haunted House* was not a happy experience for anyone. Joi Lansing was suffering from botched surgery that would eventually lead to her untimely death." Smith, Don G. *Lon Chaney, Jr.: Horror Film Star, 1906-1973*. Jefferson: McFarland & Company, Inc., Publishers, 1996.

51 *Cash Box*, January 28, 1967.

Joi found herself in the realms of grade-Z movie making and she didn't like it. The dumb blonde character had gone out of style. Joi was associated with an era gone by, and producers judged that she didn't fit the 1960s look and that she was too old to play the parts glamour girls like Elke Sommer, Ursula Andress and Raquel Welch were starring in. Confronted with the fact that she no longer could compete with the younger generation, Joi worked even harder to keep her body in tiptop shape. Her physical appearance had always been her meal-ticket and she believed that, by taking good care of her herself, she could prolong her career.

Always smiling in public and keeping up her appearance, on the inside Joi felt miserable and depressed. It was a difficult time in her life. The loss of her grandfather proved too much to overcome. Her abortions left her with an emotional scar, especially because she desperately wanted to have a child of her own. She was almost 38 and was still playing the sexpot. How long could she keep up with staying young and beautiful? What else did she have? She knew she could sing and act, but her whole career was solidly built on her sexy image. She was horrified with the thought that one day it would be over, only because she lost her looks. Looking back on her achievements in showbusiness, she told Charles Champlin, reporter for the *Los Angeles Times*, "I was always known as a glamour girl and categorized only as that. It was very limiting. I was held back by my image. You have to have some image to get established but once you're in and they realize you're part of the business, they forget about the rest of it. Many gals in the industry have more talent than they're given credit for. Looks have a lot to do with it. My being blonde and curvy, you might say, was a kind of mixed blessing."[52]

On Monday, January 24, 1967, she made the scene in the Windy City to view a new Scopitone location there. The premiere of *Hillbillys in a Haunted House* was held in Louisville, Kentucky on May 15, simultaneous with multiple openings in the Redstone Circuit of theatres in that area. Joi made public appearances at two of the houses that evening. She turned down another part, that of Venus De Marco, when it was offered to her in the summer of 1967. Jayne Mansfield had been the first choice for the part, but when she died in a car accident in June, director Stuart E. McGowan unsuccessfully offered the role to Mamie Van Doren, Diana Dors and Joi. Eventually, buxom British starlet Sabrina took the part in *Ice House* (1969).

---

52 *Los Angeles Times*, February 24, 1967.

In August, Joi visited her mother in Hollywood, and while in California, got vocal training and worked out in the gym to be in good shape for her nightclub act. She told her mother that her marriage to Stan had become strictly platonic, and that this was one of the reasons she had decided to move to Cleveland. The other reason was that she wanted to be with her new lover, Lenny 'Red' Luxemburg. Before she traveled to Ohio, she was one of the guests when George Raft was honored at a special Friar's Roast. Gathered to pay tribute were Red Buttons, Bobby Darin, Henry Fonda, Glenn Ford, George Jessel, Walter Winchell, Dean Martin and Frank Sinatra.

Joi had known Lenny Luxemburg since 1964, when she performed at his hotel, The Versailles. He lived in Shaker Heights, an inner-ring streetcar suburb of Cleveland, abutting the eastern edge of the city's limits. In the 1960s it was the richest community in the United States. Gary Lorig knew Lenny, because he had played with his pop group at The Versailles several times. "I was playing in a group called 'December's Children,' and after a gig one night we went to Leo's Casino, which was a very famous club at the time. Everybody would play at this particular club: Stevie Wonder, The Temptations, The Four Tops. One night me and my girlfriend were going to see the late show of The Temptations, and as we were walking in, Lenny was coming out with this gorgeous blonde. Lenny and I talked and then he said, 'I want you to meet miss Joi Lansing.' Normally I have no problems talking, but I was speechless. I looked at this lady, and I still remember — I was a young kid, just seventeen — she was all in white. She had the platinum hair, beautiful pure skin. It was like there was a white aura around her, like somebody was trying to protect her. She looked like an angel, she was just stunning. And I met a lot of pretty women before, with the band and everything, but this lady was above and beyond. I told her I enjoyed watching her in *Love That Bob!* and she kind of smiled, she was very shy. She didn't talk a lot, she was kind of a shy, reserved lady. But I did try to have a conversation with her, and she smiled and was very polite. And we talked about the show, which she thought was great." After their goodbyes, Gary walked in to the show, and Joi and Lenny were going to the jazz club, The Theatrical Grill, for drinks.[53]

---

53 "The Theatrical Grill, opened in 1937, not only hosted the day's top musical stars such as Judy Garland and Dean Martin, but was also the place to score the latest gambling lines and odds on sporting events, thanks to its notorious owner Morris 'Mushy' Wexler. *The Theatrical Grill* also served as a headquarters for the famous Cleveland mobster, Alex 'Shondor' Birns." *www.clevelandhistorical.org*.

About Lenny, Gary remembered, "I didn't know his business, he was always polite to us. All the groups that came in town would stay at his hotel. When I knew him, he was probably in his mid-50s. I know Lenny was pretty jealous and protective of Joi."[54]

Edward 'Torchy' Smith[55] also met Joi in Cleveland. "My stepfather owned health food stores back in the fifties and sixties, and in those days health food stores were hardly around. Joi used to promote Tiger's Milk, that was a product my stepfather carried. I used to work at his store on weekends when I went to College and during the Summer. One day, Joi walked in wearing a sweater or blouse and you could see her nipples. Nobody in Cleveland walked around like that, so every eye was on her. I waited on her, I think she had a juice. People were looking in the windows and I don't think anybody knew who she was. Nobody wore a blouse like that. Everybody was staring. I was eighteen and I was just floored. In my opinion Joi was very nice, very professional, just a very nice person. She said she was from California, but she didn't say she was a movie star or anything like that. As soon as she walked out, my mother told me she'd recognized her." Edward continued, "Every time she came in she had one of those juices where you put vegetables in; nowadays people make them at home. In those days, you could only get them at health food stores. I think she came in two or three times and then we would deliver to her. She was into all types of health food products that you could only buy at a health food store. I didn't know who she was at first and when I talked to her she told me that Bob Cummings was the one that turned her on to health foods. Every once in a while, a movie star would come into the store, because they couldn't get it anywhere else. Barbra Streisand actually came in when she played in Cleveland for a couple of weeks."[56]

Edward recalled the kind of guy Lenny was. "My father in law ran around with a pretty fast crowd, I mean a real fast crowd. He was very well known. He and my uncle on my wife's side, Jack Payner, were friends with some guys who belonged to the Jewish mafia. In 1967, Joi lived with this guy named Red Luxemburg. I went to school with his daughter, Nancy Luxemburg. She was a year older than me. Obviously, Nancy didn't like Joi. I couldn't believe that guy was living with her. Because we had to deliver, that's how I knew. My father in law was friends with him, they played tennis together. Luxemburg hung around

---

54 Source: telephone interview 07-07-2017.

55 Mr. Smith hosts a radio show: *www.babyboomerstalkradio.com*

56 Source: telephone interview 04-30-2017.

with guys from the Cleveland mafia. He owned a downtown hotel and there was a nightclub in that hotel. Luxemburg lived in a big home, I'm not sure what his business was, but he was a pretty fast guy and he hung around with the Jewish crowd. He knew mobster Shondor Birns, who was the head of the Jewish mafia."[57]

Life with Lenny had been fun for as long as it lasted. Joi didn't want to be a kept woman and after a couple months of living in the fast lane, she decided to return to the West Coast to move in with Stan. In her book, Alexis Hunter mentions the assumed reason for the break-up with Lenny. "Joi had dated him for a while, but things had not worked out the way he wanted. He was much more interested in her than she was in him. Which didn't make him happy at all. She never told me what caused the breakup, but I can't imagine her as a gangster's moll. Judy Holliday had played the part very well, but Joi was way too bright and definitely had a mind of her own. That was probably the reason it ended."[58]

Joi continued to tour the country with her new nightclub act. In August and September, she played the swank Edgewater Beach Hotel in Chicago. "I have a very well-rounded nightclub act, please excuse the pun. At first the act was very sexy. I wore extremely inviting, daring gowns. Now I'm still glamorous but not so daring. Glamorous but legit. Not too low-cut, but enough to know I'm there. The act has everything. Sex, pathos, special material." On December 3, she was named "Miss Armed Forces Day of the World" for 1967 by the B'nai B'rith at the Ambassador Hotel's nightclub, the Cocoanut Grove, on Wilshire Boulevard in Los Angeles.[59] At their luncheon, she headed an all-star show with a medley of songs. The event was taped and channeled over Armed Forces Radio & Television Services to all countries where U.S. and Allied Forces were stationed.

---

57 Source: telephone interview 04-30-2017.

58 Hunter, Alexis. *Joi Lansing ~ A Body to Die For. A Love Story*. Albany: Bear Manor Media, 2015.

59 The oldest Jewish service organization in the world, B'nai B'rith states that it is committed to the security and continuity of the Jewish people and the State of Israel and combating antisemitism and bigotry.

Scopitone, 1966.

French lobby card for *Marriage on the Rocks*.

With boxer Eddie Machen, May 1965.

Joi chatting with Dean Martin, on the set of *Marriage on the Rocks*, 1965.

German lobby card for *Marriage on the Rocks*.

Joi at the Lansing Fire Department, January 20, 1966.

The Beverly Hillbillies, Joi wears a $1400 gold lamé gown, January 29, 1966.

A playful Joi. COURTESY OF ALEXIS HUNTER

Career Opportunities

The new year proved to be a difficult year for Joi. Her new manager Lee Wolfberg tried to get her assigned for film work, but all Joi was seen in were guest appearances on TV's *The Beverly Hillbillies* and *Petticoat Junction*. How she supposedly got her part in the latter, a tv guide wrote a somewhat nasty piece: "Joi Lansing is getting more and more shots on this show because she and an executive are closerthanthis. Plus which she has talent and the biggest boobs in town." These degrading comments hurt her. Still, she never showed her annoyance when she fulfilled her "movie star duties." On April 24, she was at hand as a member of the jury for a mixed cocktail drink contest at the Beverly Hills Hotel in Los Angeles. On June 28, she appeared on the talk show of Mike Douglas and on July 1, a ravishingly beautiful Joi makes a guest appearance on *The Steve Allen Show*. But, as said before, looks are deceiving. Joi kept her inner-demons to herself, well hidden behind the mask of the professional entertainer.

In July, she was the date of friend Trini Lopez, who performed at the Greek Theater in Los Angeles, where Joi was rehearsing for a new musical play. In between TV appearances, she starred as the gold-digging blonde Lorelei Lee in a dinner theatre production of *Gentlemen Prefer Blondes*, in Memphis, in October and November. Joi had several musical numbers and got to sing "Bye Bye Baby," "A Little Girl from Little Rock," "It's Delightful Down in Chile," "Diamonds Are a Girl's Best Friend," "Gentlemen Prefer Blondes," and "Button Up with Esmond." Her co-star Bob Brooks had also appeared in the 1966 run of the show with Jayne Mansfield. The show ran for eight weeks.

Lauren Angelich, then a teenager, knew the Los Angeles apartment building where Joi lived by herself for a while. "Joi lived on La Cienega, actually right around the corner. It was a high rise with doormen, a front desk who would call a special phone in your apartment to tell you who would like to come and see you and whether they were allowed to come up. It was a wild building regarding the doorman; half of them were pimps and the other half were drug pushers! It also was a place where a lot of movie stars lived while they were in transition; they didn't know where they were going or they were going to buy a home, whatever. I used to ride the elevator up with Cary Grant because Dyan Cannon lived there. Susan Hayward, Diahann Carroll, on and on." Lauren also met Joi when visiting the building. "Joi did seem sad, but really, she was so lovely, skin like porcelain and sweet. Not a phony in any way."[60] Ice skater turned actress Nancy Czar also lived in the apartment building on La Cienega. She remembered meeting Joi in the hallways and in the elevator. Nancy remembers her as "a very pleasant person."[61]

Bill Marx, the adopted son of comedian Harpo Marx, had done the musical arrangements for her nightclub act and had become a friend. "We constantly shared our senses of humor together, and I will remember her always for what a very kind and honest person she was. We never spoke of her inner demons, nor did I ever notice in my five or six-year relationship with her any kind of malice toward anyone. I believed that she just desperately needed acceptance from the extremely difficult and often lonely professional world she had chosen for herself in which to participate. I shall remember her being both blessed and cursed by her beauty, yet to me, remaining the naturally kind and honest lady she always was."[62]

In his autobiography, Bill speaks about a friend who had attempted suicide, and how he was just in time to stop him. Bill experienced a similar situation with Joi. "Incidentally, years later, I was faced with a similar 'cry for help' from a gal I met and became good friends with from a time she did a TV commercial with Dad. She was a sweet, beautiful, big busted, sexy blonde named Joi Lansing, who worked a lot in the industry as an actress, but she always thought *only* because of her looks. She did have reasonable objectivity. One day I followed a trail of blood from her living room into the bathroom. Fortunately, I got to her just in time… Unfortunately, whether it was true, only in her imagination, or both, never was she to overcome the insecurity that plagued her."[63]

Bill comments, "I came to her apartment to rehearse. The door was unlocked, and as I walked in, I noticed a trail of blood on the white carpet leading to her bathroom. I found her conscious and called the paramedics. I believe that she had taken some serious pills that made her whoozy and affected her balance which caused her to hit her head on the corner of the living room built-in bar, and that created the blood trail. As I recall,

60 Source: email contact with author.

61 Source: email contact with author.

62 Source: email contact with author.

63 Marx, Bill. *Son of Harpo Speaks*. Duncan: Bear Manor Media, 2010.

she remained in a daze till the paramedics got there and took her to the hospital. We never did speak of that incident."[64]

In December Joi flew to Las Vegas, at the request of Frank Sinatra, to see him perform at Caesar's Palace. In January 1969, columnist Harrison Carroll wrote, "Only a few weeks ago Joi Lansing told me that she had definitely decided to get the divorce from husband Stan Todd. But she and Stan acted lovey-dovey at Stefanino's." For the 1969 season of *The Dean Martin Show*, she joined friend Dean and former lover Sid Caesar in a skit as a girl who has been saved from suicide by Sid. She cited Dean as her favorite performer to work with. "He makes everyone around him relaxed because he's so relaxed; and he works so hard, even though he looks like he's not."[65] Joi had been engaged in an affair with Sid Caesar after she broke up with Sinatra. The affair ended because Sid was married at the time and Joi was looking for a man to end her loneliness, which he couldn't provide for.

The Beverly Hillbillies.

It was Stan who accompanied Joi to the set of *Bigfoot*. The movie was shot in February 1969, at Griffith Park, Los Angeles. In *Bigfoot*, biker Christopher Mitchum and his girlfriend Judy Jordan venture off to the woods for some necking. They come across a burial ground and find a hairy creature buried in one of the plots and then suddenly are attacked themselves. Christopher tries to find help but the local police don't believe him and it takes two traveling salesmen who say they are interested in lending a hand. John Carradine and John Mitchum believe his story and think that if they can capture one of the creatures, they will be rich. The creatures have Judy tied to a stake along with Joi. Joi had crashed in the woods with her airplane and was captured by the beasts. The girls figure out that Bigfoot wants to mount them and get them

64 Source: email contact with author.

65 *Schenectady Gazette,* August 16, 1969.

pregnant because a smaller and more human looking creature keeps sniffing about. When Joi is taken up the hill as a prize for the biggest Bigfoot, she is rescued in the nick of time by Christopher, the two salesmen and the biker gang.

Christopher Mitchum recalls, "I worked with Joi for one day on *Bigfoot*. I rescued her, put her on the back of my bike, and headed down the mountain, so I really didn't get to know her at all. The shoot was in February. We were to shoot in Tehachapi, but heavy rains (flooding) started and it rained through the entire shoot. The shoot was two weeks long. They rented Hollywood Studios on Hollywood Blvd., I believe, brought in dirt and trees, and nearly the entire thing was done indoors. If there was a break in the rain, we ran up to Hollywood lake and picked up some exterior shots. As the 'star,' I revived $500 a week. I had $2,900 in overtime by the end of the first week. They didn't pay it, so I went to Screen Actors Guild. SAG told me the company could only pay 10¢ on the dollar or couldn't finish the picture. I accepted that and my character was written out of the ending of the film (which is why I rode down the hill!). A few months later, I went to a meeting (as I had a share in the film) and the investors where told why they had seen no returns on their million-dollar investment! $1 million? I'd be surprised if they spent more than $100k on that film. So, you tell me how Bob Slatzer and Tony Cardoza were driving new Cadillacs."[66]

Writer James Gordon White recalled the making of *Bigfoot*: "Joi Lansing was in. They got Joi Lansing because I insisted the girl that they had wasn't right. Cardoza [the movie's producer], you could give him a million dollars to do a movie and he'd screw it up! That's being truthful; that's not sour grapes. He had a terrible leading lady, so she got bumped down to the second lead. They got Joi Lansing, which was an improvement, and name value. She wasn't a huge name, but for a little B movie it was okay."[67]

On the set of *Bigfoot* Joi met the twenty-two-year old aspiring actress Nancy Hunter. Nancy had a bit part as one of the female creatures. The two women became instant friends and were soon inseparable. Joi introduced Nancy to comedian and talk show host Joey Bishop, and the two of them decided that the young girl didn't look like a 'Nancy' but more like a 'Rachel.'

---

66 Source: email contact with author.

67 Albright, Brian. *Wild Beyond Belief! Interviews with Exploitation Filmmakers of the 1960s and 1970s.* Jefferson: McFarland & Company, Inc., Publishers, 2008.

Joi was very happy when she was asked to do a summer musical/comedy production in New York. She was signed for *Burlesque Follies* by producer Sol Richmond to replace actress Denise Darcel after he had seen Joi on *The Dean Martin Show* earlier that year. Richmond was very happy with his new leading lady, "Burlesque comedians are a touchy breed, and I needed someone to gel. I turned on the TV set and there she was — beautiful, could sing, could dance."[68] She was signed for a salary of $2,250 a week, for a three-week engagement.

Joi and Rachel arrived in New York in June. Rehearsals took several weeks and on her days off Joi took Rachel to see the city. What started as a friendship between the two women had developed into a romance. Joi had never experienced a same-sex relationship before. To avoid a scandal, Rachel was introduced as her babysister. Stan didn't mind having Rachel around. He was glad that Rachel kept Joi company and that she made Joi happy. Both Stan and Joi knew that the marriage was over, but they had decided to stay together.

Burlesque Follies of '69 aka *Follies Burlesque '69* opened on July 31 at the Wedgewood Dinner Theater in Glen Cove, Long Island. The last performance at the Wedgewood was on August 16. When the show went on tour it started off in Latham, New York. Originally scheduled at the Colonie Summer Theatre in Latham for an engagement of only one week, *Follies Burlesque '69* was presented at the 3,000-seat theater from Sunday August 17 through Sunday the 24th of August. Extra performances were added, starting August 26 through 31. Performances were at 8:30 p.m. Tuesday through Thursday and Sunday. And eight and eleven p.m. Friday and Saturday. The last performances were in Princeton, New Jersey September 2 through 7. The musical revue starred Jayne Mansfield's ex-husband and former Mr. Universe Mickey Hargitay, who was the show's emcee. Comedian/dancer Will B. Able, singer Frank Silvano and "Miss Topless USA," Ann Patt were also seen in this production. For the Latham show stripper/actress Lily St. Cyr was billed.

"Burlesque is to spoof, to make fun of," Joi explained. "It's suggestive, not overt. Even the one stripper does an artistic job." In the same interview, she enthusiastically described Mickey Hargitay as "gorgeous!"[69] Rachel was the babysitter for Mariska and Zoltan Hargitay while their father was on stage. Alexis remembered from that time, "Mickey Hargitay was a real gentleman. They worked well together. When we were together, we

---

68 *Schenectady Gazette,* August 16, 1969.

69 *Schenectady Gazette,* August 16, 1969.

didn't hang out with any of the other performers. We lived a very private and secluded life, and a very happy life."[70]

Joi was aware of the fact that if her love affair with Rachel became known, it would ruin her career. To keep up her heterosexual image, she kept dating men. Trini Lopez was one of the men she held dates with for a couple of years. "I remember she'd just show up. Sometimes at my performances or she would call me on the phone. Especially here in Palm Springs, because this is a very small town. Every once in a while, we get together to have a dinner or drinks. She was very light-hearted, nothing serious, she got a long with me really great. I got along with her really great too," Trini recalls. "We always had a good time, I remember that she was very friendly. She was very easy to be with, very comfortable to be with. I lived in Palm Springs in 1966 and I go to know her here too. And I met Joi then and also met one of her sisters. [According to Alexis Hunter this was in 1971]. Joi didn't look her age, she looked much younger. She looked like she was in her late twenties."[71]

Follies Burlesque was a smash hit. The audiences came in droves to see the show. There was a great cross-section of types in the audience. Busloads of senior citizens seemed to find the evening an enjoyable one. Smartly dressed couples out on the town had excellent seats and roared with laughter all through the program. A review for the show read, "The current *Follies Burlesque* at Colonie this week and next leaves no holds, backscratchers or powder puffs barred. Joi Lansing and Mickey Hargitay stop at nothing to keep their avid audiences agog and aghast at the activities in the center ring. Burlesque styled skits, dances and actions leave nothing to the sexual imagination of the watchers. They love and laugh until the tears roll down their faces."[72]

One newspaper criticized the show for not bringing back the nostalgia of the days of burlesque, but rather being a mix of a burlesque show and a nightclub variety show. The review read in part, "*Follies Burlesque '69* begins in the nostalgic vein, with Joi Lansing leading some chronics in a song that pays tribute to the stars who grew up in burlesque theater. But it soon drops this motif, and before the first act has ended we have heard some contemporary and Broadway songs sung by Miss Lansing. It is pleasant enough but it does not fit into the burlesque concept." Nevertheless, reviewer Howard Healy mentions that, "One new

---

70 Source: email contact with author.

71 Source: telephone interview with author, 06-01-2017.

72 *Schenectady Gazette,* August 22, 1969.

burlesque act is the dancing of Will B. Able which, along with the singing of Frank Silvano, are among the brightest things all evening. Silvano's songs are mostly contemporary too, there's nothing wrong with that in itself (just as Miss Lansing's fresh Hollywood glamour is preferred to the hardened stereotype of a burlesque queen), but still the division is there: a good variety show and a good burlesque show mixed together but competing with one another."[73]

Another review described that, "Joi Lansing is appropriately costumed for her activities in eye-splitting effects. She accompanies her suggestive songs in a spirit of dimpled fun and with delighted wriggles. Joi starts off in a black velvet drape with her group of 'sex belles' in a number called 'Burlesque is a Stamping Ground,' then sings a few popular songs." The writer of the article continued, "Perhaps the greatest thing about burlesque is watching the people in the front row. Last night there were wonderful people in the front rows all the way around. When Miss Lansing and her sex belles moved into that old favorite, 'Scratch My Back,' complete with darling little back scratchers, they were able to recruit willing arms without going any further than the front row. It did seem, though, that some of the girls had picked people from the back rows and went racing up the aisles to capture their willing prey. Once the boys shared the stage with their individual sex belles, the amateur performances rounded out the bill."[74]

Joi's spirit was lifted with the success she experienced with *Follies Burlesque*. Her romance with Rachel was a match made in heaven, and she was over the moon because she had signed to do a play in Las Vegas.

---

73 *The Times Record,* August 21, 1969.

74 *Schenectady Gazette,* August 20, 1969.

Nightclub performance, 1969.

The Dean Martin Show, with Dean and Sid Caesar, 1969.

Joi with Judith Jordan in *Bigfoot,* 1969.

Chapter 5: The Seventies

Private Times

In the late 1960s and the early 1970s, hippies, flower power and free love dictated the sign of the times. Anti-Vietnam and anti-Nixon demonstrations illustrated the political climate. Joi, a product of the 1940s and 1950s, had a difficult time adjusting to this new age. Her morals were those of post-war America. "I saw *Hair* a couple of years ago and I wasn't ready for it. I didn't like it at all. I guess I was a real prude then, but I may have softened a little. I don't know that I am now. I had been raised very strictly in the Mormon religion and I always will be terribly 'Americanized,' I'm very patriotic. And when I saw people making fun of America, it struck me the wrong way. I have no intention of ever seeing *Oh, Calcutta*, or things like that." In defense of the new times, and with her same-sex relationship in mind, she added, "My opinion is, the loosening of these tied-up emotions that we've lived with all these years, will unthaw us. Maybe we'll be happier in the long run. People will be less uptight."[1]

With the death of Marilyn Monroe in 1962 and Jayne Mansfield in 1967, Joi and Mamie Van Doren were the last of the blonde bombshells of the 1950s who tried to keep up their sex symbol image. While Mamie was doing nude layouts in men's magazines, Joi held on to her image of the glamorous All-American girl. She was happy with a new assignment that emphasized her sexy reputation.

Late in December 1969, Joi left for Las Vegas, where she would perform the play *Come Blow Your Horn*. Neil Simons' autobiographical play had become a smash success on Broadway and ran for two years after opening in 1961. Joi remarked in an interview, "The current obscenities, the four-letter words and all that, that's another subject. I'm in a very good comedy right now, in so-called Sinful Las Vegas, and we turn people away every night. Yet we have no four-letter words to offer, no topless showgirls, merely a good script by a master writer, Neil Simon, and a well-acted comedy."[2]

1 *Men's Digest*, July 1970.

2 *Men's Digest*, July 1970.

Joi was extremely happy that she was cast for this production. "Stan Selden, producer of the Thunderbird shows in Las Vegas has given me a wonderful opportunity to do my first legitimate comedy role in *Come Blow Your Horn*. And I love every minute of it. Working before a live audience is like hitting the jackpot. I'm hoping to do much more of the same type work in years to come."[3] The cast received their lines beforehand and everybody knew their lines when they went in rehearsal. Rehearsals took ten days.

The play's story is about an older brother who coaches his younger brother in the ways of love, despite the interference of their parents and other complications. In showing his kid brother Buddy (Ron De Salvo) how to live it up, Alan (Billy Hayes) sets up a date for him with the blonde beauty living upstairs, Peggy Evans (Joi). Alan assures the youngster, "the ball's already over the fence. All you've got to do is run the bases." In her scenes with Ron De Salvo, Joi looked sensational in a knitted "net" dress. Ron remembered, "It was an interesting cast. Bill Hayes was the male lead. My character is the lead of the entire play, but he was kind of the handsome, older guy. Bill was a well-known singer and stage performer. At that time, I'd never met anyone who loved what he did and loved to be in front of an audience, more than Bill Hayes. He was at that stage of his career where he wasn't sure about what the next step was. What is so wonderful about Bill is that right after the show ended, he ended up getting a role in one of the most famous soap operas in the country and he became a huge star for the next 45 years in television. The older guy in the show was Jackie Coogan. He was kind of a crusty guy. And then a woman who became a very good friend, Selma Diamond. Who was a very famous comedian, but more of a writer than she was a comedian. She did many television shows. Getting on the stage was not the easiest thing for her. She had never been to Las Vegas, she was out of her element, but was delightful. We all became really good friends. It was a very nice ensemble." Ron continues, "I think of all the cast members, that Jackie Coogan was the most aloof. He really didn't have a lot to do with us. He was a very famous guy for a long time when he was a little boy and then he became kind of overweight, bald, not particularly attractive. I think it annoyed him. I think he probably had an ego that was well beyond where he was at that time. He was a much bigger star at one point, than being in an ensemble show in a Las Vegas casino. The rest of us just loved what we were doing.

"In 1970, it was the beginning of Vegas bringing Broadway shows to the Casino's. This was a new trend. Now they do it all the time, but then

---

3   *Men's Digest,* July 1970.

it was rare. They cut it to 90 minutes, so there's no intermission, so that people don't leave, you know, go gamble. They tried to make the dialogue if they can, as racy as they can, with sexual innuendos, which they would not do in New York on stage. Neil Simon would not have written that, the way we've played it, which was fun. It was fun, because that's what the audience came to see. They came to see a little bit of a racy attitude they wouldn't be able to see in Los Angeles or anywhere else." Ron remembers working with Joi. "I'm the young ingenue, the young boy and she's this buxom blonde and this would be my first sexual experience. Not physical, but emotional sexual experience. There's a moment, whether it was in the original script or not, where my face ends up between her breasts. That probably was staged more for Las Vegas. I think it is inherent in the play. I remember it being a very fun moment on stage. Even if it's on stage, there always is a little chemistry that has to go on between the players. And I think that's why the show was quite a big hit at the time. Everybody loved it and it was packed every night. I think it had a lot to do with the people that were in it, but mostly Joi. I think Joi was the big star."[4]

Come Blow Your Horn.

The play was scheduled for five weeks, opening at the Thunderbird's Continental Theater. One preview read in part, "Neil Simon's explosively funny Broadway comedy hit, "Come Blow Your Horn,' which opened at the Thunderbird Hotel Christmas Eve, promises to be Las Vegas' new remedy for ailing funny bones. Producer Stan Selden has gathered some of the most talented personalities in show business for his second T-Bird production. Heading the cast are veteran actor Jackie Coogan, blonde bombshell Joi Lansing, Selma Diamond and Billy Hayes. Completing the lineup are attractive Kerry Slattery and Ron De Salvo."[5]

4 Source: telephone interview with author, 01-24-2018.

5 *Vegas Visitor*, 1969.

Bill Hayes kept the notes he wrote after the show had ended. "Richard Vath was our director for *Come Blow Your Horn*, and his cast came in as a big winner. I enjoyed playing that fast-talking Hal March role. Most of my scenes were with the facile Ron and the busty Joi and the edible Kerry [Slattery], and I enjoyed those a lot. They all were happy to have the job and did their utmost to play the scaled-down (90-minute one-act) version

Come Blow Your Horn, with Ron De Salvo, 1969.

of the play and to do right by Neil Simon's funny yet pithy lines. Selma [Diamond], for some strange reason, seemed more interested in showing off her new Bill Blass hat and playing the nickel slot-machines in the casino than in actually improving her part; she seemed to believe that it was only her nasal voice that made the lines funny rather than the savory wit and inherent comment put there by the author. Jackie Coogan was another case entirely. He apparently was lowering himself to appear in our play, was unhappy from the first rehearsal to the closing night final show, slept backstage between his scenes, and offered no energy or attempt at performance level when he was onstage. The play was cut to conform to Las Vegas standard show-length, but it was still a heck of a play and could have been better than it was. We played two shows a night — eight pm and midnight — for two weeks. Then the Thunderbird changed our schedule to four pm and eight pm shows. Business was better that way, and it also gave us actors a chance to see other shows. Since we were currently performing at the Thunderbird, most hotels would 'comp' us. We saw, among others, (all free!) Juliet Prowse and Anthony Newley, Roger Williams, Jay Lawrence, Kathryn Grayson and Howard Keel, Marty May, Babette Bardot, Bobby Sherwood, Jackie Gayle, Wayne Cochran, Allan Drake, Zsa Zsa Gabor, Sandy Baron, Boyce and Hart, Gail Martin, Edie Adams, Lainie Kazan, Vic Damone, Rich Little, Paul Anka and Dean Martin! We went to see the Elvis Presley Show, had waited through 'The World's Greatest Authority' Professor Irwin Corey, and then they came to our banquette and told us we were not to be 'comped,' but that we'd each have to come up with $25 to stay and see Elvis do his thing. I didn't have that much, so I left just as the curtain was being raised on the charismatic man in the white jumpsuit. Sorry I missed that!"[6]

Bill remembers Joi lovingly. "She was a very classy person, I thought. She was a good actress, very cooperative. She had this tremendous bust and when she stood up when being introduced in a hotel, she got quite a surprising round of applause. But she was much more than that. She was not just a body, she had a good acting talent and she did the part quite well. She was funny, sweet, warm. She was a heck of a person."[7]

Ron De Salvo became a close friend. "Joi, who everybody loved, was very famous in Hollywood, everybody knew her. After the show, when we had our night off, she and I and Alex became kind of like a threesome, we just became inseparable. We had such a nice time together and I'll never forget that after the show we went to have drinks with Dean Martin. We did things that you would never be able to do with anybody else. Everybody loved Joi and loved being around her so much, that they welcomed her. I remember one of the greatest experiences in my entire life, was going with Joi and Alex to the comeback of Elvis Presley. We were there on his opening night and we're sitting in the front row — because it was Joi — and then afterwards we went backstage to meet Elvis Presley. That's just one of the moments in my life that I will never forget as long as I live. It was all because of Joi Lansing.

"We did stay in touch after the show, but there's something about the theater where you become so connected while you're all together. When it's over, as much as you want to stay connected, everybody goes on to other shows and so you do kind of disappear from each other more than you expected to or wanted to. We stayed in touch for a while and then got

---

6 Used with permission by Mr. Hayes.

7 Source: telephone interview with author, 01-23-2018.

out of touch and then I remember hearing that she passed away. She was so adored by everybody. Men adored her because she was the bombshell, but even women liked her, because she was very gentle, a very gentle soul and she was not intimidating to anybody. She had such a great heart that I think that even women, who would be competitive, allowed her. Just being who she was. Joi is a lovely name for her."[8]

Rachel accompanied Joi to Vegas. "I stayed in Joi's dressing room while she was on stage, ready to help with her hair and three costume changes when she rushed in between scenes. The play lasted about an hour-and-a-half, including a short intermission, and the audience absolutely loved it! *Come Blow Your Horn* was a smashing success! Congratulatory telegrams to Joi came from all over the country. Her mother, Virginia, even sent a telegram addressed to both of us. I had met her a few times when we were in L.A. when she'd come to visit Joi at her apartment. Even then, though rather cool with Joi, she was very gracious to me. I don't think she ever suspected the depth of our relationship but was happy that Joi had a friend to keep her company."[9]

Through her mother, Joi got the news that her half-brother Larry had divorced his wife Janey Lorraine Powell, whom he had married in 1959. Joi hadn't been in contact much with Larry the last years, but on the news of his divorce she immediately took up contact with him.

After her five-week stint in Las Vegas, Joi contacted her former press agent, Bill Corcoran. "I last heard from Joi in 1970 when she wrote me asking if I might be able to get her a booking at one of the big nightclubs in Chicago. I wasn't able to get her booked anywhere. As I recall, her asking price was $2,500 a week."[10] She was considered by Russ Meyer, who was known for writing and directing a series of successful sexploitation films that featured campy humor, sly satire and large-breasted women, to appear in *Beyond the Valley of the Dolls* (1970) and director Roger Corman wanted her for his production of *The Big Doll House* (1971), but because of the cruelty and nudity in the scripts she backed off.

"Of course, I'm also concerned about all this talk of the star system being out. The buildups from the big studios are so important. That's where it is, that's where everybody gets their start. Today, it's pretty much of a different story. You have to create your own energy, so to speak. You have to go out and do it yourself. And it's no easy task, believe me," Joi

---

8 Source: telephone interview with author, 01-24-2018.

9 Hunter, Alexis. *Joi Lansing — A Body to Die For. A Love Story*. Albany: Bear Manor Media, 2015.

10 Source: email contact with author.

told a reporter in an interview for *Men's Digest* magazine. She decided to take her career in her own hands and started working on a self-produced stage show. She had picked out the songs she wanted to sing and was talking things over with Stan and Rachel. "I'm very excited now about a revue I'm putting together. It may be the start of a second nightclub career for me." She added, "You've got to surround yourself with talented

The cast of *Come Blow Your Horn*.

people; with managers who know what they're doing — with agents who are right in there, in the swim of things. For instance, in this revue I'm putting together I've got to go out myself and find the talent for the revue: the comics, the dancers and the musicians. I'm very thankful that I've had a background in nightclubs. That'll make it easier for me, because I know where to find what I'm looking for. I know where it's at as far as music is concerned. I'll do the lead singing, and I'll have another singer in the show as well. I'll have a feature dancer, a couple of comedians, and whatever else it takes. The musicians, however, will be very important because I won't have a big 30-piece orchestra, only about seven pieces and I want them all to be able to do something special."[11]

11 *Men's Digest*, July 1970.

Joi made the rounds to keep herself in the spotlight, making personal appearances on talk shows. As a teenager, Craig Marin met Joi twice, on a New York TV show around 1969 and again approximately one year later. "The two times I met Joi were on the set of a popular long-running New York–tri-state area show, *Joe Franklin's Memory Lane*. It was a talk show with a very nostalgic stance. Joe had hundreds of stars on his show, ranging from folks like Arthur Tracey, the Street Singer to Butterfly McQueen to Shelley Winters to…Joi Lansing. In my early to mid-teens my friend Paul and I did a Laurel & Hardy act, where we dressed up like them and did a skit. Joe's people heard about us and asked us to appear. On one of our appearances, Joi was also on. On another appearance, about a year later, we were on talking about Laurel & Hardy films as ourselves, and again Joi was also on. At fifteen, it was 'oh wow. Mrs. Superman!' At 16, it was 'wow! What a beautiful, kind and gentle person she is. And so well built! In person, whew!'"[12]

Joi and Rachel moved to New York. At first, they stayed at the South-Central Park Hotel and later at an apartment building, Parc V at 785 Fifth Avenue. During their stay in the city Joi arranged a sitting with glamour photographer Maurice Seymour. Alexis remembered, "She, like many celebrities, had a photo shoot and then took the photos to Duplicate Photo in Hollywood and had hundreds printed up. I was with her at her last photo session in New York, and she paid Seymour something like $500 for the session and prints."[13] Some of the photos Seymour shot were rather risqué with Joi in a see through dress and topless, holding her hands before her breasts. Always refusing to take it all off for photos or film, Joi had noticed the change of times and told one interviewer, "I'm ready to take it all off. As soon as someone asks me; for film that is. Originally, I said that anyone can take off their clothes. But in these times keeping them on is a real talent. I still feel that way. But there's no point getting uptight about it. I've proven over and over again that I can get good parts and more than enough work, while keeping it on. Let's put it this way, I originally said that the day Barbra Streisand or Tom Jones agree to do nude films, that's when I'll relent. Well, I understand Barbra is now going to do a nude scene, so I guess I'm ready. I hope they have a big enough lens, you know."[14]

Joi and Rachel left New York when Stan bought a house in Palm Springs, on Tuscan 2460. The women moved in with Stan. Besides

---

12 Source: email contact with author.

13 Source: email contact with author.

14 *Men's Digest*, July 1970.

the house in Palm Springs, they also shared an apartment at Mariner's Village — 13802 North West Passage — in Marina del Rey. During her stay in New York, Joi had noticed a pain in her breast and contacted a doctor upon her return to Los Angeles. After a few weeks, she learned that the pain was caused by a cancerous tumour, and in the Summer of 1970, she had to undergo surgery at St. John's Hospital in Santa Monica. Leslie Todd remembered, "I did know about her illness right from the beginning. I had been going to nursing school in 1968-1969 and Stan would always call me and ask me questions. Questions about everything. Medications, tests, X-rays and surgeries were all foreign to him and very frightening. He was very devastated. Joi had hoped the surgery would remove all the cancer and she would be fine, but it had already spread too far by that time."[15]

Recuperating took a long time and Joi did not feel well enough to work. Rachel was just a 23-year-old girl when she experienced the agony her lover was in during this time. Joi was very depressed and tried to take her own life. Rachel had to hide away her medication, to make sure she didn't take all the pills at once. Joi's dependency on her medication and sleeping pills, combined with the use of alcohol, didn't help the depression to go away, but made her sad and depressed feelings grow worse. With her health deteriorating, she lost her grip on life and after extensive use of alcohol, on reality. "It was imperative that she get the sleep she needed to look as good as she could on film. Sadly, I was soon to discover one of her secrets. She suffered from terrible depression and would drink to ease the pain and then take a Seconal or two to go to sleep. When that didn't work, she'd wake up and take a few more pills. I tried to stop her, but she became infuriated and did as she pleased."[16]

Rachel had a hard time convincing her to stay strong and keep fighting. Luckily the chemo made her feel better after a while and Joi thought of taking up her career again. She signed with NBC to make an appearance in, what proved to be her last TV series, *The Governor and J.J.*, which aired on December 16. A newspaper column mentions that, "Joi Lansing, makes her first TV appearance in a long time. She's a sight for all men's eyes in a white sweater and mini skirt."

In 1971, Joi was asked to replace actress June Wilkinson for a dinner-theatre production of *Pajama Tops* at the Alhambra Dinner Theatre in Jacksonville, Florida, because June had other obligations to fulfil at that time.

---

15 Source: email contact with author.

16 Hunter, Alexis. *Joi Lansing ~ A Body to Die For. A Love Story*. Albany: Bear Manor Media, 2015.

As with other dinner theaters of the 1970s, Alhambra initially relied on the appeal of former stars of film, television and music to attract customers. They earned weekly pay between $1,500 and $5,000 for six to eight weeks as well as being able to enjoy the weather and amenities in Florida. Entertainment Producer of the Alhambra, Tod Booth, Sr. mentioned, "When their careers cooled, a star could learn a show and take it on the dinner theater circuit. That one show could be a meal ticket for a year or two."[17]

Actor Bill Dolive rehearsed with Joi, Jack R. Marks and Del Hinckley. Bill remembered working with Joi, but because of her illness had little time to get to know her. "Quite honestly I have little memory of Joi. I think we only rehearsed for a week and that was about 45 years ago. All I can say is she seemed quite nice. My memories of the nasty folks are always more vivid!"[18] June Wilkinson recalled, "I did know Joi Lansing before she was going to do *Pajama Tops*. In fact, I recommend her for the part. I was busy doing *The Marriage-Go-Round* with Louis Jordan and I did not finish the run until *Pajama Tops* was a couple of days into rehearsals. None of us knew how sick Joi was at the time. Halfway through rehearsals she got too sick and had to quit. The theatre called and asked me to help them out since I knew the show and had already worked with some of the actors. They knew I could be ready for opening night, so I agreed to take her place. Bless her heart, she died soon after."[19]

Although Joi did very little work toward the end of her life, Alexis remembers the last two years were happy ones. The chemotherapy seemed to be working, soothing the pain. She had stopped taking pills and minimized the use of alcohol. The two women spent a lot of time together. Stan, who lived in the same house, kept to himself, saying he couldn't cope seeing Joi in the state she was in. Virginia also hardly visited her daughter. The care for Joi solely belonged to Rachel. It was a very private time. No one in the business knew she was ill.

---

17 Source: Wikipedia.

18 Source: email contact with author.

19 Source: email contact with author.

Joi with Jackie Coogan, Las Vegas, 1969.

Joi with singer Bobby Vinton and music promoter Pete Bennett. Las Vegas, 1969.

Joi and Craig Marin, 1969. COURTESY OF CRAIG MARIN

Joi and Rachel aka Alexis Hunter, 1971.

Joi with Bill Dolive (right) and the rest of the cast of *Pajama Tops*, 1971. COURTESY OF BILL DOLIVE

The End

In July 1972, Joi was scheduled to star in a new production of *Follies Burlesque* at the Meadowbrook Theatre in New Jersey. She never made it into rehearsals, because on July 1, Joi was admitted to the hospital again, suffering from severe anaemia. On August 7, 1972 at 10:30 pm, with only Rachel at her side, Joi Lansing died in St. John's Hospital in Santa Monica. She was 43 years old.

On August 11, her services were held in Santa Paula, California. Roy Wilson Sr., a Christian Science reader, conducted the services and delivered the eulogy. Her mother, brother Larry and other family members attended the funeral. *Bigfoot* director Bob Slatzer, Del Nebeker, Jr., George E. Wilson, P.C. Nelson, Royden Rice and Allen Briscoe were the pallbearers. Frank Sinatra sent flowers. There were also several federal agents present at Joi's funeral, because of the death threats Bob F. Slatzer had received for his book in which he revealed he secretly married Marilyn Monroe and his accusations that Marilyn was murdered by the Kennedys. Furthermore, the funeral ceremonies were overshadowed by the fact that Joi's mother insisted that her daughter would be buried. Joi herself had wanted to be embalmed and put in a mausoleum. Virginia refused to pay for the ceremony and in the end, didn't pay at all. Stan Todd had to pay for the funeral. Alexis states, "Virginia and Stan fought over who was going to pay for her funeral. They ignored her wishes, ignored what I had to say. It was an ongoing fight between the two of them. It was terrible. I was a kid with no money and had no status as her lover. This did not exist in 1972. I had no power."[20]

Ron De Salvo was the only one to send Alexis a note after Joi's passing. "She told me I was the only one sending her a note, telling her how sad it made me and that I couldn't even imagine what she was going through. It was hard for me to believe that I was the only one sending a note. That didn't make sense." Ron wasn't aware of the nature of Alexis' relationship with Joi. "No, not at all. I actually thought they

---

20   Source: email contact with author.

were sisters. It was logical, they took care of each other and I wouldn't have thought anything else. But no matter what, she had lost a part of her..."[21]

Joi is buried at Santa Paula cemetery, plot 444, section N. On the certificate of death Joi's date of birth was inadvertently mentioned as April 6, 1934. On Wednesday, August 29, her will was filed in Superior Court. Her entire estate was left to her husband.

John Shupe once again experienced his aunt Virginia's harshness. "I received a phone call from her shortly after Joi died. She was angry with me for an obituary I had written for *The Salt Lake Tribune* and *Ogden Standard Examiner*. I was working as a stringer providing general news stories and photos to those two newspapers. Since I had a copy of Joi's birth certificate in my family files I wrote a local obituary. I had no idea my story contained information different from what she was giving out to the press in California. Joi's date of birth was changed over the years to make Joi appear younger than she really was, in an attempt to extend her career."[22]

Columnist and friend Ken Mayer concluded his obituary with the following text, "Like every other gal with a whistle-getting figure, Joi wanted most to be recognized for her ability to act and sing. And like her predecessors, Harlow, Monroe and Mansfield, her public demanded of her body rather than her mind. Nor did she ever delude herself into thinking otherwise, for she was well aware that her physical attributes were no small part of her success. In truth, she both recognized and resented the fact, but wisely chose not to fight it. But with a face and form like hers, her straight dramatic and vocal talents never had a chance. So many times, she scored the 'near miss,' and so few times the 'hit,' that it seemed almost as though she was predestined to be runner-up to the main event, but never to win it. Yet she never gave up in her pursuit. There's something almost extra tragic about the passing away of one who seemingly has no right to die. And it becomes even more so, when the deceased was gifted with so strong a desire to live. But life, like the fate of man, is a totally unpredictable factor and chooses, for the recipients of death, as indiscriminately as it bestows the gift of birth. Last week it chose Joi Lansing for death. By her own standards, she had never begun to live."[23]

21 Source: telephone interview with author, 01-24-2018.

22 Source: email contact with author.

23 *Boston Herald,* Aug. 15, 1972.

Carlton Wasmansdorf, who died in 1975 and Joi's mother, who passed away on New Year's Day 1984, were buried next to Joi. Carlton had divorced Virginia in 1975. Despite being a multi-millionaire, he gave all his assets and wealth to a university in California. He left no money to Virginia nor anyone else in his family. Stan Todd died at age 67 in Los Angeles in his sleep, on December 17, 1985. He never remarried. His daughter Leslie passed away unexpectedly on September 28, 2018, from a heart-attack.

Alexis Hunter picked up the pieces of her life. Devastated with her loss she left California and moved in with her parents. She now lives near Palm Springs, cherishing the memories of her relationship with Joi and she makes sure that the love of her life will not be forgotten.

When a Girl's Beautiful, publicity photo, 1947.

Filmography

When A Girl's Beautiful
Columbia Pictures, 1947
68 minutes — Black and white
PRODUCER: Wallace MacDonald. **DIRECTOR:** Frank McDonald.
SCREENPLAY: Brenda Weisberg. *Based on the story by* Henry K. Moritz.
MUSIC: Joseph Dubin and Lyle Murphy. **EDITOR:** Jerome Thoms.
PHOTOGRAPHY: Henry Freulich. **SOUND:** Russell Malmgren.

CAST: Adele Jergens *(Adele Jordan)*; Marc Platt *(Johnny Hanley)*; Patricia White *(Ellen Trennis)*; Stephen Dunne *(Marshall Forrest)*; Steven Geray *(Stacy Dorn)*; Mona Barrie *(Cordova)*; Jack Leonard *(Jack Leonard; himself)*; Paul Harvey *(Stafford Shayne)*; Lela Bliss *(Betty Broadway)*; Nancy Saunders *(Sue Dennis; a model)*; Doris Houck *(Ginger Munday; a model)*; Amelita Ward *(Bunty McGregor; a model)*; Peggy Call *('Koko' Glayde)*; Vera Stokes *(Sherry Hutton; a model)*; Lucille Casey, Charmienne Harker, Dorothy Huff, **Joy Loveland** *(Models, the Temptation Girls)*.

Linda Be Good
Eagle Lion, 1947
67 minutes — Black and white
PRODUCER: Matty Kemp. **DIRECTOR:** Frank McDonald.
SCREENPLAY: George Halasz and Leslie Vale. *Based on the story by* Howard Harris and Richard Irving Hyland. **MUSIC:** Jack Mason.
EDITOR: Norman E. Cerf. **MAKE-UP:** Paul Malcolm. **COSTUMES:** Marie Donovan. **PHOTOGRAPHY:** George Robinson. **SOUND:** Ferrol Redd.

CAST: Elyse Knox *(Linda Prentiss)*; John Hubbard *(Roger Prentiss)*; Marie Wilson *(Margie LaVitte)*; Gordon Richards *(Sam Thompson)*; Jack Norton *(Jim Benson)*; Ralph Sanford *(Nunnally LaVitte)*; Claire Carleton *(Myrtle)*; Allan Nixon *(Officer Jones)*; Anne Beck, Marilyn

Chase, Karen X. Gaylord, Charmienne Harker, Dorothy Huff, **Joy Loveland**, Martha Montgomery, Edna Ryan, Marjorie Stapp, Ruth Valmy *(Showgirls, the Cameo Girls)*.

Tex Williams and His Western Caravan
(Musical Short #12-G)
Universal International, 1947
15 minutes — Black and white
PRODUCER: Will Cowan. **DIRECTOR:** Will Cowan.

CAST: Tex Williams *(Himself)*; Deuce Spriggins *(Himself)*; Smokey Rogers *(Himself)*; Western Caravan Band *(Themselves)*; Patricia Alphin, Dorothy Huff, **Jill Lansing** *(The Texas Trio)*.

The Counterfeiters
20th Century Fox, 1948
74 minutes — Black and white
PRODUCER: Maurice H. Conn. **DIRECTOR:** Peter Stewart. **SCREENPLAY:** Fred Myton and Barbara Worth. *Based on the story by* Maurice H. Conn. **MUSIC:** Irving Gertz. **EDITOR:** Martin G. Cohn and Harry Coswick. **PHOTOGRAPHY:** James S. Brown. **SOUND:** John Carter.

CAST: John Sutton *(Inspector Jeff MacAllister)*; Doris Merrick *(Margo Talbot)*; Hugh Beaumont *(Philip Drake)*; Lon Chaney *(Louie Struber)*; George O'Hanlon *(Frankie Dodge)*; Douglas Blackely *(Tony Richards)*; Herbert Rawlinson *(Norman Talbot)*; Pierre Watkins *(Carter)*; Don Harvey *(Dan Taggart)*; Fred Coby *(Piper)*; **Joyce Lansing** *(Caroline, an Art Model)*; Gerard Gilbert *(Jerry McGee)*.

Easter Parade
Metro Goldwyn Mayer, 1948
107 minutes — Color
PRODUCER: Arthur Freed. **DIRECTOR:** Charles Waters. **SCREENPLAY:** Sidney Sheldon, Frances Goodrich and Albert Hackett. *Based on the story by* Frances Goodrich and Albert Hackett. **MUSIC:** Conrad Salinger. **EDITOR:** Albert Akst. **MAKE-UP:** Jack Dawn. **HAIR STYLES DESIGNER:** Sydney Guilaroff. **WOMEN COSTUMES:** Irene. **MEN COSTUMES:** Valles. **PHOTOGRAPHY:** Harry Stradling. **SOUND:** Douglas Shearer.

CAST: Judy Garland *(Hannah Brown)*; Fred Astaire *(Don Hewes)*; Ann Miller *(Nadine Hale)*; Peter Lawford *(Jonathan Harrow III)*; Jules Munshin *(Headwaiter François)*; Clinton Sundberg *(Mike, the Bartender)*; Lola Albright *(Hat Model)*; **Joy Lansing** *(Hat Model)*; Shirley Ballard, Pat Van Iver, Ruth Hall, Marjorie Jackson, Gail Langford, Elaine Sterling, Patricia Walker *(Showgirls)*; Lynn & Jean Romer *("Delineator" Twins)*.

The girls from *Easter Parade*, 1948.

Julia Misbehaves
Metro Goldwyn Mayer, 1948
99 minutes — Black and white
PRODUCER: Everett Riskin. DIRECTOR: Jack Conway. SCREENPLAY: Monckton Hoffe and Gina Kaus. *Based on the novel "The Nutmeg Tree"* by Margery Sharp. MUSIC: Adolph Deautsch. EDITOR: John Dunning. MAKE-UP: Jack Dawn. HAIR STYLES DESIGNER: Sydney Guilaroff. COSTUMES: Eugene Joseff. PHOTOGRAPHY: Joseph Ruttenberg. SOUND: Douglas Shearer and Charles E. Wallace.

CAST: Greer Garson *(Julia Packett)*; Walter Pidgeaon *(William Sylvester Packett)*; Peter Lawford *(Ritchie Lorgan)*; Elizabeth Taylor

(Susan Packett); Cesar Romero *(Fred Ghenoccio)*; Lucille Watson *(Mrs. Packett)*; Fritz Feld *(Pepito)*; Phyllis Morris *(Daisy)*; Veda Ann Borg *(Louise)*; Elaine Sterling, Lola Albright, Shirley Ballard, **Joy Lansing**, Ruth Hall, Marjorie Jackson, Gail Langford, Patricia Walker *(Mannequins)*.

Super Cue Men
Metro Goldwyn Mayer, 1949
9 minutes — Black and white
PRODUCER: Pete Smith. **DIRECTOR:** David Barclay. Script: Joe Ansen. **EDITOR:** Joseph Dietrik.

CAST: Jimmy Caras, Willie Mosconi, **Joy Lansing**, Corinne Calvet and Pete Smith *(Narrator)*.

Take Me Out to the Ballgame
Metro Goldwyn Mayer, 1949
93 minutes — Color
PRODUCER: Arthur Freed. **DIRECTOR:** Busby Berkeley. **SCREENPLAY:** Harry Tugend and George Wells. *Based on the story by* Gene Kelly and Stanley Donen. **MUSIC:** Roger Edens and Conrad Salinger. **EDITOR:** Blanche Sewell. **MAKE-UP:** Jack Dawn. **HAIR STYLES DESIGNER:** Sydney Guilaroff. **WOMEN COSTUMES:** Helen Rose. **MEN COSTUMES:** Valles. **PHOTOGRAPHY:** George Folsey. **SOUND:** Douglas Shearer.

CAST: Frank Sinatra *(Dennis Ryan)*; Esther Williams *(K.C. Higgins)*; Gene Kelly *(Eddie O'Brien)*; Betty Garrett *(Shirley Delwyn)*; Edward Arnold *(Joe Lorgan)*; Jules Munshin *(Nat Goldberg)*; Richard Lane *(Michael Gilhuly)*; Tom Dugan *(Slappy Burke)*; Virginia Bates *(Girl on Train)*; **Joy Lansing** *(Girl on Train)*.

The Barkleys of Broadway
Metro Goldwyn Mayer — 1949
109 minutes — Color
PRODUCER: Arthur Freed. **DIRECTOR:** Charles Walters. **SCREENPLAY:** Betty Comden and Adolph Green. **MUSIC:** Lenny Hayton. **EDITOR:** Albert Akst. **MAKE-UP:** Jack Dawn. **HAIR STYLES DESIGNER:** Sydney Guilaroff. **PHOTOGRAPHY:** Harry Stradling. **SOUND:** Douglas Shearer.

CAST: Fred Astaire *(Josh Barkley)*; Ginger Rogers *(Dinah Barkley)*; Oscar Levant *(Ezra Miller)*; Billie Burke *(Mrs. Livingstone Belney)*; Gale Robbins *(Shirelene May)*; Jacques François *(Jacques Pierre Barredout)*; George Zucco *(The Judge)*; Clinton Sundberg *(Bert Felsher)*; Inez Cooper *(Pamela Driscoll)*; Carol Brewster *(Gloria Amboy)*; Claire Carleton *(Marie)*; Mimi Doyle *(Actress)*; Betty Jane Howarth and **Joy Lansing** *(Girls in Theater)*.

Neptune's Daughter
Metro Goldwyn Mayer, 1949
95 minutes — Color
PRODUCER: Jack Cummings. DIRECTOR: Edward Buzzell. SCREENPLAY: Dorothy Kingsley. MUSIC: Leo Arnaud and George Stoll. EDITOR: Irvine Warburton. MAKE-UP: Jack Dawn. HAIR STYLES DESIGNER: Sydney Guilaroff. COSTUMES: Irene. PHOTOGRAPHY: Charles Rosher. SOUND: Douglas Shearer and Ralph A. Pender.

CAST: Esther Williams *(Eve Barrett)*; Red Skelton *(Jack Spratt)*; Ricardo Montalban *(José O'Rourke)*; Bett Garrett *(Betty Barrett)*; Keenan Wynn *(Joe Backett)*; Xavier Cugat *(Himself)*; Ted de Corsia *(Lukie Luzette)*; Mike Mazurki *(Mac Mozolla)*; Mel Blanc *(Pancho)*; Elaine Sterling *(Miss Pratt)*; **Joy Lansing** *(Linda, a Bathing Suit Model)*; Dorothy Abbott, Bette Arlen, Sue Casey, Diane Gump, Jackie Hammette, Lonnie Pierce *(Models)*; G. Pat Collins *(Detective)*; Theresa Harris *(Matilda the Maid)*.

The House of Tomorrow
Metro Goldwyn Mayer, 1949
7 minutes — Color/Black and white
PRODUCER: Fred Quimby. DIRECTOR: Tex Avery. Story: Jack Cosgriff and Rich Hogan. MUSIC: Scott Bradley. ANIMATORS: Walter Clinton, Michael Lah and Grant Simmons.

CAST: Frank Graham (Narrator), Don Messick (Narrator), **Joy Lansing** (Bathing Beauty on Television).

The Girl from Jones Beach
Warner Bros., 1949
78 minutes — Black and white
PRODUCER: Alex Gottlieb. **DIRECTOR:** Peter Godfrey. **SCREENPLAY:** I.A.L. Diamond, *based on a story by* Allen Boretz. **MUSIC:** David Buttolph. **EDITOR:** Rudi Fehr. **MAKE-UP:** George Bau and Gordon Bau. **HAIR STYLIST:** Alma Armstrong. **PHOTOGRAPHY:** Frank Bjerring. **SOUND:** Dolph Thomas.

CAST: Ronald Reagan *(Bob Randolph aka Robert Benerik);* Virginia Mayo *(Ruth Wilson);* Eddie Bracken *(Chuck Donovan);* Dona Drake *(Connie Martin);* Henry Travers *(Judge Bullfinch);* Lois Wilson *(Mrs. Wilson);* Florence Bates *(Miss Emma Shoemaker);* Jerome Cowan *(Mr. Graves, Ruth's Attorney);* Helen Westcott *(Miss Brooks);* Paul Harvey *(Jim Townsend);* Myrna Dell *(Lorraine Scott);* Lola Albright *(Vickie);* Carol Brewster, Lorinne Crawford, Karen X. Gaylord, **Joy Lansing**, Vonne Lester, Betty Underwood, Nancy Valentine, Joan Vohs, Alice Wallace *(Randolph Girls);* Eve Whitney *(Penelope).*

In The Good Old Summertime
Metro Goldwyn Mayer, 1949
102 minutes — Color
PRODUCER: Joe Pasternak. **DIRECTOR:** Robert Z. Leonard. **SCREENPLAY:** Samson Raphaelson, *based on the play by* Miklos Laszlo. **MUSIC:** George Stoll and Robert Van Eps. **EDITOR:** Adrienne Fazan. **MAKE-UP:** Jack Dawn and Dorothy Ponedel. **HAIR DESIGNER:** Sydney Guilaroff. **PHOTOGRAPHY:** Jerome Hester. **SOUND:** Charles E. Wallace.

CAST: Judy Garland *(Veronica Fisher);* Van Johnson *(Andrew Delby Larkin);* S.Z. Sakall *(Otto Oberkugen);* Spring Byington *(Nellie Burke);* Clinton Sundberg *(Rudy Hansen);* Buster Keaton *(Hickey);* Marcia Van Dyke *(Louise Parkson);* Lillian Bronson *(Aunt Addie);* Liza Minnelli *(Daughter);* Bette Arlen *(Pretty Girl);* **Joy Lansing** *(Pretty Girl);* Jack Roth *(Orchestra Leader).*

Key to The City
Metro Goldwyn Mayer, 1950
101 minutes — Black and white
PRODUCER: Z. Wayne Griffin. DIRECTOR: George Sidney.
SCREENPLAY: Robert Riley Crutcher, *based on a story by* Albert Beich.
MUSIC: Bronislau Kaper. EDITOR: James E. Newcom. MAKE-UP: Jack Dawn. PHOTOGRAPHY: Ed Hubbell. SOUND: Conrad P. Kahn and Douglas Shearer.

CAST: Clark Gable *(Steve Fisk)*; Loretta Young *(Clarissa Standish)*; Frank Morgan *(Fire Chief Duggan)*; Marilyn Maxwell *(Sheila, the 'Atom' Dancer)*; Raymond Burr *(Les Taggart)*; James Gleason *(Sergeant Hogan)*; Lewis Stone *(Judge Silas Standish)*; Raymond Walburn *(Mayor Billy Butler)*; Pamela Britton *(Miss Unconscious)*; Bridget Carr *(Miss Dream Girl)*; Dorothy Ford *(Miss Construction)*; **Joy Lansing** *(Miss Garbage Truck)*; Victor Sen Yung *(Chinese MC)*.

Holiday Rhythm
Lippert Pictures, 1950
58 minutes — Black and white
PRODUCER: Irving Kay and Jack Leewood. DIRECTOR: Jack Scholl.
SCREENPLAY: Lee Wainer. MUSIC: Bert Shefter. EDITOR: Lou Hesse.
MAKE-UP: Otis Malcolm. PHOTOGRAPHY: Benjamin Kline. SOUND: Tommy Thompson and Frank Webster.

CAST: Mary Beth Hughes *(Alice)*; David Street *(Larry Carter)*; Wally Vernon *(Klaxon)*; Tex Ritter *(Himself)*; Alan Harris *(Mr. Superdyne)*; Donald MacBride *(Earl E. Byrd)*; Sid Melton *(Himself)*; Tommy Noonan *(Surgeon)*; Peter Marshall *(Orderly)*; Regina Day *(Dancer)*; Vera Lee *(Dancer)*; Tommy Ladd *(Dancer)*; Lynn Davis *(Dancer)*; Gloria Grey *(Singer)*; George Arnold's Rhythm on Ice Show *(Ice Show Performers)*; **Joy Lansing** *(Showgirl)*.

Pier 23
Lippert Pictures, 1951
58 minutes — Black and white
PRODUCER: William Berke and Jack Leewood. DIRECTOR: William Berke. SCREENPLAY: Julian Harmon and Victor West. MUSIC: Bert Shefter. EDITOR: Carl Pierson and Harry Reynolds. MAKE-UP: Paul Stanhope. PHOTOGRAPHY: Jack Greenhalgh. SOUND: Glen Glenn.

CAST: Hugh Beaumont *(Dennis O'Brien)*; Ann Savage *(Ann Harmon)*; Edward Brophy *(Professor Shicker)*; Richard Travis *(Police Inspector Lieutenant Bruger)*; Margia Dean *(Flo Klingle)*; Mike Mazurki *(Ape Danowski)*; David Bruce *(Charles Giffen)*; Raymond Greenleaf *(Father Donovan)*; Eve Miller *(Norma Harmon)*; Harry Hayden *(Doctor Earl J. Tomkins)*; **Joy Lansing** *(Cocktail Waitress)*.

On The Riviera
20th Century Fox, 1951
89 minutes — Color
PRODUCER: Sol C. Siegel. DIRECTOR: Walter Lang. SCREENPLAY: Valentine Davies, Phoebe and Henry Ephron, *based on a play by* Hans Adler and Rudolph Lothar. MUSIC: Earle Hagen, Cyril J. Mockridge and Alfred Newman. EDITOR: J. Watson Webb Jr. MAKE-UP: Ben Nye. PHOTOGRAPHY: Leon Shamroy. SOUND: Roger Heman and E. Clayton Ward.

CAST: Danny Kaye *(Jack Martin/Henri Duran)*; Gene Tierney *(Lili Duran)*; Corinne Calvet *(Colette)*; Marcel Dalio *(Philippe Lebrix)*; Jean Murat *(Felix Periton)*; Henri Letondal *(Louis Foral)*; Joyce MacKenzie *(Mimi)*; Monique Chantal *(Minette)*; Clinton Sundberg *(Antoine)*; Sig Ruman *(Gapeaux)*; Mari Blanchard *(Eugenie)*; **Joy Lansing** *(Marilyn Turner)*; Ellen Ray *(Specialty Dancer)*; Tyra Vaughn *(Specialty Dancer)*; Gwen Verdon *(Specialty Dancer)*.

FBI Girl
Lippert, 1951
74 minutes — Black and white
PRODUCER: William Berke and Jack Leewood. DIRECTOR: William Berke. SCREENPLAY: Dwight Babcock and Richard Landau, *based on a story by* Rupert Hughes. MUSIC: Darrell Calker. EDITOR: Phil Cahn. MAKE-UP: Del Armstrong. PHOTOGRAPHY: Jack Greenhalgh. SOUND: John Carter.

CAST: Audrey Totter *(Shirley Wayne)*; Cesar Romero *(Glen Stedman)*; George Brent *(Jeff Donley)*; Tom Drake *(Carl Chercourt)*; Raymond Burr *(Blake)*; Raymond Greenleaf *(Governor Owen Grisby)*; Margia Dean *(Natalie Craig)*; Don Garner *(Paul Craig)*; Alexander Pope *(George Denning)*; Tommy Noonan *(Television Act)*; Peter Marshall *(Television Act)*; Jan Kayne *(Doris)*; **Joy Lansing**

(Susan); Walter Coy *(Priest);* Byron Foulger *(Morgue Attendant);* Suzanne Ridgway *(Waitress).*

Two Tickets to Broadway
RKO, 1951
106 minutes — Color
PRODUCER: Howard Hughes, Norman Krasna and Jerry Wald.
DIRECTOR: James V. Kern. **SCREENPLAY:** Sid Silvers and Hal Kanter, *based on a story by* Sammy Cahn. **MUSIC:** Walter Scharf. **EDITOR:** Harry Marker. **MAKE-UP:** Mel Berns. **PHOTOGRAPHY:** Edward Cronjager and Harry Wild. **SOUND:** Clem Portman and Earl Wolcott.

CAST: Tony Martin *(Dan Carter);* Janet Leigh *(Nancy Peterson);* Gloria DeHaven *(Hannah Holbrook);* Eddie Bracken *(Lew Conway);* Ann Miller *(Joyce Campbell);* Barbara Lawrence *(Foxy Rogers);* Suzanne Ames, Joan Barton, Carol Brewster, Shirley Buchanan, Gwen Caldwell, Rosalee Calvert, Mara Corday, Jane Easton, Barbara Freking, Patricia Hall, Nora Hayden, Marilyn Johnson, Joanne Jordan, Shirley Kimball, Lucy Knoch, Mona Knox, **Joy Lansing**, June McCall, Vera Miles, Angela Stevens, Shirley Tegge, Mamie Van Doren, Linda Williams, Joan Whitney *(Showgirls).*

Two Tickets to Broadway, with Tony Martin and Janet Leigh, 1951.

Singin' In The Rain
MGM, 1952
103 minutes — Color
PRODUCER: Arthur Freed. **DIRECTOR:** Stanley Donen and Gene Kelly. **SCREENPLAY:** Betty Comden and Adolph Green. **MUSIC:** Lenny Hayton. **EDITOR:** Adrienne Fazan. **MAKE-UP:** William Tuttle, Ben Lane, John True and Dorothy Ponedel. **PHOTOGRAPHY:** Harold Rosson. **SOUND:** Norwood A. Fenton.

CAST: Gene Kelly *(Don Lockwood)*; Donald O'Connor *(Cosmo Brown)*; Debbie Reynolds *(Kathy Selden)*; Jean Hagen *(Lina Lamont)*; Millard Mitchell *(R.F. Simpson)*; Cyd Charisse *(Dancer)*; Douglas Fowley *(Roscoe Dexter)*; Rita Moreno *(Zelda Zanders)*; Dawn Addams *(Teresa)*; Elaine Stewart *(Lady in Waiting)*; Tommy Farrell *(Sid Phillips)*; Kathleen Freeman *(Phoebe Dinsmore)*; Lance Fuller *(Chorus Boy)*; Tommy Walker *(Chorus Boy)*; Diane Garrett *(Usherette)*; Jan Kayne *(Usherette)*; Dorothy Patrick *(Usherette)*; Judy Landon *(Olga Mara)*; **Joy Lansing** *(Girl in Audience)*; Sylvia Lewis *(Female Tango Dancer)*; Anne Neyland *(Chorus Girl)*; Norma Zimmer *(Chorus Girl)*.

Glory Alley
MGM, 1952
76 Minutes — Black and white
PRODUCER: Nicholas Nayfack. **DIRECTOR:** Raoul Walsh. **SCREENPLAY:** Art Cohn. **MUSIC:** Georgie Stoll. **EDITOR:** Gene Ruggiero. **PHOTOGRAPHY:** William H. Daniels. **SOUND:** Robert B. Lee.

CAST: Ralph Meeker *(Socks Barbarrosa)*; Leslie Caron *(Angela)*; Kurt Kasznar *(The Judge)*; Gilbert Roland *(Peppi Donnato)*; John McIntire *(Gabe Jordan)*; Louis Armstrong *(Shadow Johnson)*; Jack Teagarden *(Himself)*; Pat Goldin *(Jabber)*; John Indrisano *(Spider)*; Mickey Little *(Domingo)*; Joan Barton, Barrie Chase, **Joy Lansing**, Beryl McCutcheon, Erin Selwyn, Eve Whitney *(Showgirls)*.

The Merry Widow
MGM, 1952
105 minutes — Color
PRODUCER: Joe Pasternak. **DIRECTOR:** Curtis Bernhardt.
SCREENPLAY: Sonya Levien and William Ludwig. **MUSIC:** Jay

Blackton. EDITOR: Conrad A. Nervig. MAKE-UP: William Tuttle.
PHOTOGRAPHY: Robert Surtees. SOUND: Douglas Shearer.

CAST: Lana Turner *(Crystal Radek)*; Fernando Lamas *(Count Danilo)*; Una Merkel *(Kitty Riley)*; Richard Haydn *(Baron Popoff)*; King Donovan *(Nitki)*; Lisa Ferraday *(Marcella)*; Gwen Verdon *(Specialty Dancer)*; Bette Arlen, Geneviève Aumont, Toni Carroll, Sue Casey, Perdita Chandler, Zina d'Harcourt, Patricia Edwards, Anne Kimbell, Judy Landon, **Joy Lansing**, Meredith Leeds, Marilyn Malloy, Wanda McKay, Ann Roberts, Sally Seaver, Gale Sherwood, Greg Sherwood, Gene Summers, Beverly Thompson *(Girls at Maxim's)*.

The French Line
RKO, 1953
102 minutes — Color
PRODUCER: Howard Hughes and Edmund Grainger. DIRECTOR: Lloyd Bacon. SCREENPLAY: Mary Loos and Richard Sale, *based on a story by* Matty Kemp and Isabel Dawn. MUSIC: Walter Scharf. EDITOR: Robert Ford. MAKE-UP: Mel Berns. PHOTOGRAPHY: Harry Wild. SOUND: Clem Portman and Earl Wolcott.

CAST: Jane Russell *(Mary Carson)*; Gilbert Roland *(Pierre DuQuesne)*; Arthur Hunnicutt *('Waco'Mosby)*; Mary McCarty *(Annie Farrell)*; Joyce MacKenzie *(Myrtle Brown)*; Rita Corday *(Celeste)*; Barbara Darrow *(Donna Adams)*; Barbara Dobbins *(Kitty Lee)*; Suzanne Alexander, Virginia Bates, Shirley Buchanan, Sue Casey, Jane Easton, Anne Ford, Charmienne Harker, Joyce Johnson, **Joy Lansing**, Jarma Lewis, Dolores Michaels, Jean Moorhead, Kim Novak, Dawn Oney, Gloria Pall, Shirley Patterson, Pat Sheehan, Dolly Summers, Shirley Tegge, Beverly Thompson, Gloria Watson, Doreen Woodbury.

So You Want to Go to a Night Club
Warner Bros., 1954
10 minutes — Black and white
PRODUCER: Richard L. Bare. DIRECTOR: Richard L. Bare. SCREENPLAY: Richard L. Bare, *based on a story by* Dean Riesner. MUSIC: William Lava. EDITOR: Rex Steele. PHOTOGRAPHY: John MacBurnie. SOUND: Edwin B. Levinson.

CAST: George O'Hanlon *(Joe McDoakes)*; Jane Frazee *(Alice McDoakes)*; Del Moore *(Homer)*; Philip Van Zandt *(Pierre, the Headwaiter)*; **Joy Lansing** *(Lorna Lamour)*; Ralph Brooks *(Bandleader)*; Leon Alton, Steve Carruthers, Luis Delgado *(Club Patrons)*; Jack Chefe *(Waiter)*; Joe Ploski *(Nightclub Chef)*; Brick Sullivan *(Policeman in Conga Line)*.

So You Want to Go to a Nightclub, 1954.

So You're Taking in a Roomer
Warner Bros., 1954
10 minutes — Black and white
PRODUCER: Richard L. Bare. DIRECTOR: Richard L. Bare.
SCREENPLAY: Richard L. Bare, *based on a story by* George O'Hanlon.
MUSIC: William Lava. EDITOR: Rex Steele. PHOTOGRAPHY: Ellsworth Fredericks. SOUND: Edwin B. Levinson.

CAST: George O'Hanlon *(Joe McDoakes)*; Jane Frazee *(Alice McDoakes)*; Rodney Bell *(Marvin Schultz)*; Steve Carruthers, James Gonzalez, Fed Kelsey, Charles Morton, Jack Mower *(Racetrack Spectators)*; Herb Vigran *(Heimie Callahan)*; Charles Sullivan *(Heimie's Henchman)*; **Joy Lansing** *(Blonde Roomer)*; Douglas Evans *(Roomer)*; Donald Kerr *(Telephone Repairman)*.

Rear Window

Paramount, 1954
102 minutes — Color
PRODUCER: Alfred Hitchcock. **DIRECTOR:** Alfred Hitchcock. **SCREENPLAY:** John Michael Hayes, *based on a short story by* Cornell Woolrich. **MUSIC:** Franz Waxman. **EDITOR:** George Tomasini. **MAKE-UP:** Wally Westmore. **PHOTOGRAPHY:** Robert Burks. **SOUND:** John Cope and Harry Lindgren. **COSTUME AND WARDROBE DEPARTMENT:** Joan Joseff.

CAST: James Stewart *(L.B. Jefferies)*; Grace Kelly *(Lisa Carol Fremont)*; Wendell Corey *(Detective Lieutenant Doyle)*; Thema Ritter *(Stella)*; Raymond Burr *(Lars Thorwald)*; Judith Evelyn *(Miss Lonelyhearts)*; Ross Bagdasarian *(Songwriter)*; Georgine Darcy *(Miss Torso)*; Sara Berner *(Woman on Fire Escape)*; Frank Cady *(Man on Fire Escape)*; Jesslyn Fax *(Miss Hearing Aid)*; Stephanie Griffin, **Joy Lansing** *(Rooftop Sunbathers)*; Sue Casey *(Sunbather)*; Marla English, Kathryn Grant *(Girls at Songwriter's Party)*; Alfred Hitchcock *(Songwriter's Clock-Winder)*.

Son of Sinbad

RKO, 1955
91 minutes — Color
PRODUCER: Howard Hughes and Robert Sparks. **DIRECTOR:** Ted Tetzlaff. **SCREENPLAY:** Jack Pollexfen and Aubrey Wisberg. **MUSIC:** Victor Young. **EDITOR:** Roland Gross and Frederic Knudtson. **MAKE-UP:** Mel Berns. **PHOTOGRAPHY:** William Snyder. **SOUND:** Clem Portman, Frank Sarver and Stanford Houghton.

CAST: Dale Robertson *(Sinbad)*; Sally Forrest *(Ameer)*; Lili St. Cyr *(Nerissa)*; Vincent Price *(Omar Khayyam)*; Mari Blanchard *(Christina)*; Leon Askin *(Khalif)*; Nejla Ates *(Dancer in Market)*; Kalantan *(Dancer in Desert)*; Dawn Oney *(Alicia)*; Suzanne Alexander, Suzanne Ames, Bette Arlen, Joanne Arnold, Carol Brewster, Shirley Buchanan, Gwen Caldwell, Sue Casey, Jane Easton, Arline Hunter, Jackie Loughery, Diana Mumby, Gloria Pall, Pat Sheehan, Doreen Woodbury *(Harem Girls)*; Roxanne Arlen, Roxann Delman, Jeanne Evans, Jonni Paris *(Arab Women)*; Diane James, Joanne Jordan, Joyce Johnson, **Joy Lansing**, Vone Lester, Evelyn Lovequist, Dolores Michaels, Kim Novak, Rosemary Webster, Trudy Wroe *(Raiders)*.

The Kentuckian
United Artists, 1955
104 minutes — Color
PRODUCER: Harold Hecht and James Hill. DIRECTOR: Burt Lancaster. SCREENPLAY: A.B. Guthrie Jr., *based on the novel by* Felix Holt. MUSIC: Bernard Herrmann and Roy Webb. EDITOR: George E. Luckenbacher. MAKE-UP: Robert Schiffer. PHOTOGRAPHY: Ernest Laszlo. SOUND: John Kean and Paul Scmutz Sr.

CAST: Burt Lancaster *(Elias Wakefield)*; Dianne Foster *(Hannah Bolen)*; Diana Lynn *(Susie Spann)*; Walter Matthau *(Stan Bodine)*; Donald McDonald *(Little Eli Wakefield)*; John McIntire *(Zack Wakefield)*; Una Merkel *(Sophie Wakefield)*; John Carradine *(Ziby Fletcher)*; John Litel *(Pleasant Tuesday Babson)*; Rhys Williams *(Constable)*; Edward Norris *(Roulette Dealer)*; Will Wright *(Shopkeeper)*; Lisa Ferraday *(Gambler)*; Lee Erickson *(Luke Lester)*; **Joy Lansing** *(scenes deleted)*.

Daddy Long Legs
20th Century Fox, 1955
126 minutes — Color
PRODUCER: Samuel G. Engel. DIRECTOR: Jean Negulesco. SCREENPLAY: Phoebe Ephron and Henry Ephron, *based on the novel by* Jean Webster. MUSIC: Cyril J. Mockridge and Alfred Newman. EDITOR: William Reynolds. MAKE-UP: Ben Nye. PHOTOGRAPHY: Leon Shamroy. SOUND: Alfred Bruzlin and Harry M. Leonard.

CAST: Fred Astaire *(Jervis Pendleton III)*; Leslie Caron *(Julie Andre)*; Terry Moore *(Linda Pendleton)*; Thelma Ritter *(Alicia Pritchard)*; Fred Clark *(Griggs)*; Charlotte Austin *(Sally McBride)*; Larry Keating *(Ambassador Alexander Williamson)*; Kathryn Givney *(Gertude Pendleton)*; Kelly Browm *(Jimmy McBride)*; Ray Anthony *(Himself)*; Sara Shane *(Pat)*; Barrie Chase, Pat Sheehan, Suzanne Alexander, Jeanne Moorhead, **Joy Lansing** *(Showgirls)*.

Finger Man
Allied Artists, 1955
82 minutes — Black and white
PRODUCER: Lindsley Parsons. DIRECTOR: Harold Schuster. SCREENPLAY: Warren Douglas, *based on a story by* Norris Lipsius

Daddy Long Legs, with Fred Astaire, 1955.

and John Lardner. **MUSIC:** Paul Dunlap. **EDITOR:** Maurice Wright. **MAKE-UP:** Ted Larsen. **PHOTOGRAPHY:** William Sickner. **SOUND:** Tom Lambert.

CAST: Frank Lovejoy *(Casey Martin);* Forrest Tucker *(Dutch Becker);* Peggie Castle *(Gladys Baker);* Timothy Carey *(Lou Terpe);* John Cliff *(Johnny Cooper);* Glenn Gordon *(Carlos Armor);* William Leicester *(Jim Rogers);* John Close *('Big' Walters);* Hugh Sanders *(Mr. Burns);* Evelyn Eaton *(Lucille Martin);* Charles Maxwell *(Fred Amory);* Lewis Charles *(Lefty Stern);* **Joy Lansing** *(Blonde in Bar);* Lisa Montell *(Bit Part).*

So You Want to be a V.P.
Warner Bros., 1955
10 minutes — Black and white
PRODUCER: Richard L. Bare. **DIRECTOR:** Richard L. Bare.
SCREENPLAY: Richard L. Bare, *based on a story by* George O'Hanlon.
MUSIC: William Lava. **EDITOR:** Leo Shreve. **PHOTOGRAPHY:** Carl Guthrie. **SOUND:** M.A. Merrick.

CAST: George O'Hanlon *(Joe McDoakes);* Steve Carruthers *(Carruthers);* Philip Van Zandt *(Spider Murphy);* **Joy Lansing** *(Secretary Miss Pointdexter);* Ralph Brooks *(Golfer/Man in Bar);* Harold Miller, Guy Way, Jack Mower *(Men in Bar);* Monty O'Grady, Murray Pollack, Norman Stevans *(Co-Workers);* Emory Parnell *(Harry Batten);* Anne O'Neal *(Mrs. Batten);* Jackson Wheeler *(Homer, Fifth Vice President).*

So You Want to be a Policeman
Warner Bros., 1955
10 minutes — Black and white
PRODUCER: Richard L. Bare. **DIRECTOR:** Richard L. Bare.
SCREENPLAY: Richard L. Bare, *based on a story by* George O'Hanlon.
MUSIC: William Lava. **EDITOR:** Leo Shreve. **PHOTOGRAPHY:** Carl Guthrie. **SOUND:** M.A. Merrick.

CAST: George O'Hanlon *(Joe McDoakes);* Jane Frazee *(Alice McDoakes);* **Joy Lansing** *(Blonde Driver);* Sandy Sanders *(Motorcycle Patrolman);* Mickey Simpson *(Police Sergeant);* James Flavin *(Police Commissioner);* Arthur Q. Bryan *(Narrator).*

So You Think the Grass Is Greener
Warner Bros., 1956
10 minutes — Black and white
PRODUCER: Richard L. Bare. **DIRECTOR:** Richard L. Bare.
SCREENPLAY: Richard L. Bare, *based on a story by* George O'Hanlon.
MUSIC: William Lava. **EDITOR:** Leo Shreve. **PHOTOGRAPHY:** Carl Guthrie. **SOUND:** M.A. Merrick.

CAST: George O'Hanlon *(Joe McDoakes)*; Jane Frazee *(Alice McDoakes)*; **Joy Lansing** *(Geraldine Backspace)*; Steve Carruthers *(Milkman)*; Ralph Brooks, James Conaty, Harold Miller *(Elevator Passengers)*; Guy Way, Murray Pollack, Monty O'Grady *(Co-Worker)*; Emory Parnell *(Joe's Boss)*.

Terror at Midnight
Republic, 1956
70 minutes — Black and white
PRODUCER: Rudy Ralston. **DIRECTOR:** Franklin Adreon.
SCREENPLAY: John K. Butler, *based on a story by* John K. Butler and Irving Shulman. **MUSIC:** R. Dale Butts. **EDITOR:** Tony Martinelli. **MAKE-UP:** Bob Mark. **PHOTOGRAPHY:** Bud Thackery. **SOUND:** Melvin M. Metcalfe Sr.

CAST: Scott Brady *(Neal Rickards)*; Joan Vohs *(Susan Lang)*; Frank Faylen *(Fred Hill)*; John Dehner *(Lew Hanlon)*; Virginia Gregg *(Helen Hill)*; Ric Roman *(Police Sergeant Brazzi)*; John Gallaudet *(George Flynn)*; Kem Dibbs *(Nick Mascotti)*; Percy Helton *(Speegie)*; Francis DeSales *(Police Lieutenant Conway)*; John Maxwell *(Police Captain Allyson)*; Rick Vallin *(Police Officer Gaudino)*; John Damler *(Police Officer Garfinkle)*; Dan Terranova *(The Kid)*; **Joi Lansing** *(Hazel)*; Doris Singleton *(Linda)*; Marjorie Stapp *(Waitress)*.

The Brave One
RKO, 1956
100 minutes — Color
PRODUCER: Frank King and Maurice King. **DIRECTOR:** Irving Rapper.
SCREENPLAY: Harry S. Franklin, Merrill and Donald Trumbo, *based on a story by* Dalton Trumbo. **MUSIC:** Audrey Granville. **EDITOR:** Merrill G. White. **PHOTOGRAPHY:** Jack Cardiff. **SOUND:** George Reid.

CAST: Michel Ray *(Leonardo)*; Rodolfo Hoyos Jr. *(Rafael Rosillo)*; Elsa Cárdenas *(Maria)*; Carlos Navarro *(Don Alejandro Videgaray)*; **Joi Lansing** *(Marion Randall)*; Fermín Rivera *(Matador)*; Jorge Treviño *(Salvador)*; Carlos Fernández *(Manuel)*; Eduardo Alcaraz *(Ticket Seller)*; Rafael Alcayde *(Señor Vargas)*; Manuel de la Vega *(Police Officer)*; Miguel Ángel Ferriz *(Father Valverde)*; Pascal Garciá Peña *(Señor Palma)*; Beatriz Ramos *(Señorita Sanchez)*; Manuel Sánchez Navarro *(Luis)*.

Hot Cars
United Artists, 1956
60 minutes — Black and white
PRODUCER: Howard W. Koch and Aubrey Schenk. DIRECTOR: Don McDougall. SCREENPLAY: Don Martin and Richard Landau, *based on the novel by* H. Haile Chace. MUSIC: Sam Waxman. EDITOR: George A. Gittens. MAKE-UP: Ted Coodley. PHOTOGRAPHY: William Margulies. SOUND: Michael Pozen.

CAST: John Bromfield *(Nick Dunn)*; **Joi Lansing** *(Karen Winter)*; Mark Dana *(Smiley Ward)*; Carol Shannon *(Jane Dunn)*; Ralph Clanton *(Arthur Markel)*; Robert Osterloh *(George Hayman)*; Dabbs Greer *(Detective Davenport)*; Charles Keane *(Lieutenant Jefferson)*; Vic Cutrier *(Bret Carson)*; John Frederick *(Hutton)*; Paula Hill *(Mrs. Davenport)*; Kurt Katch *(Otto Krantz)*; Maurice Marks *(Paul, the bartender)*; George Sawaya *(Lieutenant Holmes)*; Joan Sinclair *(Miss Rogers)*.

Hot Shots
Allied Artists, 1956
62 minutes — Black and white
PRODUCER: Ben Schwalb. DIRECTOR: Jean Yarbrough. SCREENPLAY: Jack Townley and Elwood Ullman, *based on a story by* Jack Townley. MUSIC: Arthur Morton. EDITOR: Neil Brunnenkant. MAKE-UP: Emile Vigne. PHOTOGRAPHY: Harry Neumann. SOUND: Charles Schelling and Ralph Butler.

CAST: Huntz Hall *(Horace DeBussy 'Sach' Jones)*; Stanley Clements *(Stanislaus 'Duke' Coveleskie)*; **Joi Lansing** *(Connie Forbes)*; Phil Phillips *(Joey Munroe)*; David Gorcey *(Chuck)*; Jimmy Murphy *(Myron aka Butch)*; Queenie Smith *(Mrs. Kate Kelly)*; Robert Shayne *(Pamer Moncton Morley aka Pierre)*; Mark Dana *(George Slater)*; Henry Rowland *(Karl)*; Isabel Randolph *(Mrs. Taylor)*; Myron Cook, Bess

Flowers, Philo McCullough, Gloria Pall *(Party Guests)*; Evelyn Rudie *(Annie)*; Joe Gray *(Sam)*.

Touch of Evil
Universal International, 1958
95 minutes — Black and white
PRODUCER: Albert Zugsmith. **DIRECTOR:** Orson Welles.
SCREENPLAY: Orson Welles, *based on the novel* 'Badge of Evil' by Whit Masterson. **MUSIC:** Henry Mancini. **EDITOR:** Aaron Stell and Virgil Vogel. **MAKE-UP:** Bud Westmore. **PHOTOGRAPHY:** Russell Metty.
SOUND: Lesley I. Carey and Frank Wilkinson.

CAST: Charlton Heston *(Mike Vargas)*; Janet Leigh *(Susan Vargas)*; Orson Welles *(Police Captain Hank Quinlan)*; Joseph Calleia *(Police Sergeant Pete Menzies)*; Akim Tamiroff *(Joe Grandi)*; Joanna Moore *(Marcia Linnekar)*; Ray Collins *(District Attorney Adair)*; Dennis Weaver *(Mirador Motel Midnight Manager)*; Valentin De Vargas *(Pancho)*; Phil Harvey *(Blaine)*; **Joi Lansing** *(Zita)*; Marlene Dietrich *(Tana)*; Zsa Zsa Gabor *(Strip-Club Owner)*; Eva Gabor *(Stripper)*; Joseph Cotton *(Coroner)*; Mercedes McCambridge *(Gang Leader)*; Keenan Wynn *(Bartender)*; John Dierkes *(Policeman)*.

Touch of Evil, 1958.

Queen of Outer Space
Allied Artists, 1958
80 minutes — Black and white
PRODUCER: Ben Schwalb. **DIRECTOR:** Edward Bernds. **SCREENPLAY:** Charles Beaumont, *based on the story* 'Queen of the Universe' by Ben Hecht. **MUSIC:** Marlin Skiles. **EDITOR:** William Austin. **MAKE-UP:** Emile LaVigne and John G. Holden. **PHOTOGRAPHY:** William Whitley. **SOUND:** Charles Schelling.

CAST: Zsa Zsa Gabor *(Talleah)*; Eric Fleming *(Captain Neal Patterson)*; Eric Fleming *(Captain Neal Patterson)*; Dave Willock *(Lieutenant Mike Cruz)*; Laurie Mitchell *(Queen Yllana)*; Lisa Davis *(Motiya)*; Paul Birch *(Professor Konrad)*; Patrick Waltz *(Lieutenant Larry Turner)*; Barbara Darrow *(Kael)*; Marilyn Buferd *(Odeena)*; Gerry Gaylor *(Base Commander)*; **Joi Lansing** *(Larry's Girl)*; Mary Ford, Marya Stevens, Laura Mason, Lynn Cartwright, Kathy Marlowe, Coleen Drake, Tania Velia, Norma Young, Marjorie Durant *(Venusian Girls)*.

The Fountain of Youth
Desilu Productions, 1958
27 minutes — Black and white
PRODUCER: Orson Welles and Desi Arnaz. **DIRECTOR:** Orson Welles. **SCREENPLAY:** Orson Welles, *based on the story* 'Youth from Vienna' by John Collier. **MUSIC:** Julian Davidson and Orson Welles. **EDITOR:** Bud Molin. **MAKE-UP:** Maurice Seiderman. **PHOTOGRAPHY:** Sidney Hickox.

CAST: Dan Tobin *(Humphrey Baxter)*; **Joi Lansing** *(Carolyn Coates)*; Rick Jason *(Alan Brody)*; Nancy Kulp *(Stella Morgan)*; Billy House *(Albert Morgan)*; Madge Blake, Marjorie Bennett *(Journalist)*; Orson Welles *(Host, narrator)*.

A Hole in the Head
United Artists, 1959
120 minutes — Color
PRODUCER: Frank Capra and Frank Sinatra. **DIRECTOR:** Frank Capra. **SCREENPLAY:** Arnold Schulman, *based on the play by* Arnold Shulman. **MUSIC:** Nelson Riddle. **EDITOR:** William Hornbeck. **MAKE-UP:** Bernard Ponedel. **PHOTOGRAPHY:** William H. Daniels. **SOUND:** Fred Lau.

CAST: Frank Sinatra *(Tony Manetta)*; Edward G. Robinson *(Mario Manetta)*; Eleanor Parker *(Eloise Rogers)*; Carolyn Jones *(Shirl)*; Thelma Ritter *(Sophie Manetta)*; Keenan Wynn *(Jerry Marks)*; **Joi Lansing** *(Dorine)*; Connie Sawyer *(Miss Wexler)*; James Komack *(Julius Manetta)*; Eddie Hodges *(Ally Manetta)*; Dub Taylor *(Fred)*; George DeWitt *(Mendy Yales)*; Benny Rubin *(Abe Diamond)*; Ruby Dandridge *(Sally)*; Joyce Nizzari *(Alice)*; Anne G. Sterling *(Woman at Race Track)*.

It Started with a Kiss
Metro Goldwyn Mayer, 1959
104 minutes — Color
PRODUCER: Aaron Rosenberg. DIRECTOR: George Marshall. SCREENPLAY: Charles Lederer, *based on the story by* Valentine Davies. MUSIC: Jeff Alexander. EDITOR: John McSweeney. MAKE-UP: William Tuttle. PHOTOGRAPHY: Robert Bronner. SOUND: Franklin Milton.

CAST: Glenn Ford *(Sergeant Joe Fitzpatrick)*; Debbie Reynolds *(Maggie Putnam)*; Eva Gabor *(Marquesa Marion de la Rey)*; Gustavo Rojo *(Antonio Soriano)*; Fred Clark *(Major General Tim O'Connell)*; Edgar Buchanan *(Richard Tappe)*; Harry Morgan *(Charles Meriden)*; Robert Warwick *(Congressman Muir)*; Frances Bavier *(Mrs. Tappe)*; Netta Packer *(Mrs. Muir)*; Robert Cunningham *(The Major)*; Carmen Phillips *(Belvah)*; **Joi Lansing** *(Checkroom Girl)*; Betty Koch, Pat Jones *(Models)*.

But Not for Me
Paramount, 1959
111 minutes — Black and white
PRODUCER: William Perlberg and George Seaton. DIRECTOR: Walter Lang. SCREENPLAY: John Michael Hayes, *based on the play by* Samson Raphaelson. MUSIC: Leith Stevens. EDITOR: Alma Macrorie. MAKE-UP: Wally Westmore. PHOTOGRAPHY: Robert Burks. SOUND: Harold Lewis and Charles Grenzbach.

CAST: Clark Gable *(Russell Ward)*; Carroll Baker *(Ellie Brown/Borden)*; Lilli Palmer *(Kathryn Ward)*; Lee J. Cobb *(Jeremiah MacDonald)*; Barry Coe *(Gordon Reynolds)*; Thomas Gomez *(Demetrios Bacos)*; Charles Lane *(Al Atwood)*; Wendell Holmes *(Miles Montgomery)*; Tom Duggan *(Roy Morton)*; Mike Mahoney *(Cop)*; **Joi Lansing** *(Bathing Beauty)*; Vince Williams *(Magazine Photographer)*.

The Atomic Submarine
Allied Artists, 1959
72 minutes — Black and white
PRODUCER: Alex Gordon. **DIRECTOR:** Spencer Gordon Bennet.
SCREENPLAY: Orville H. Hampton, *based on a story by* Irving Block and Jack Rabin. **MUSIC:** Alexander Laszlo. **EDITOR:** William Austin. **EDITOR:** William Austin. **MAKE-UP:** Emile LaVigne.
PHOTOGRAPHY: Gilbert Warrenton. **SOUND:** Ralph Butler and Marty Greco.

CAST: Arthur Franz *(Richard Holloway)*; Dick Foran *(Dan Wendover)*; Brett Halsey *(Carl Neilson Jr.)*; Tom Conway *(Sir Ian Hunt)*; Paul Dubov *(David Milburn)*; Bob Steele *(CPO Griffin)*; Victor Varconi *(Dr. Clifford Kent)*; **Joi Lansing** *(Julie)*; Jean Moorhead *(Helen Milburn)*; Selmer Jackson *(Admiral Terhune)*; Jack Mulhall *(Justin Murdock)*; Richard Tyler *(Frogman Carney)*; Ken Becker *(Frogman Powell)*; Sid Melton *(Chester Tuttle)*; Frank Watkins *(Watkins)*.

Inside Magoo
United Productions of America, 1960
15 minutes — Color
PRODUCER: Stephen Bosustow. **DIRECTOR:** Abe Levitow and John F. Becker. **STORY:** Al Bertino and Dick Kinney. *Live-action sequences written by* John F. Becker. **MUSIC:** Del Castillo.

CAST: Jim Backus *(Mr. Magoo/Himself)*; Stephen Bosustow *(Himself)*; Marvin Miller *(Narrator)*; Jeff Corey *(Doctor)*; **Joi Lansing** *(Nurse)*.

Who Was That Lady?
Columbia Pictures, 1960
115 minutes — Black and white
PRODUCER: Norman Krasna. **DIRECTOR:** George Sidney.
SCREENPLAY: Norman Krasna, *based on the play by* Norman Krasna.
MUSIC: André Previn. **EDITOR:** Viola Lawrence. **MAKE-UP:** Ben Lane.
PHOTOGRAPHY: Harry Stradling. **SOUND:** James Flaster.

CAST: Tony Curtis *(David Wilson)*; Dean Martin *(Michael Haney)*; Janet Leigh *(Ann Wilson)*; James Whitmore *(Harry Powell)*; John McIntire *(Bob Doyle)*; Barbara Nichols *(Gloria Coogle)*; **Joi Lansing** *(Florence Coogle)*; Larry Keating *(Parker)*; Larry Storch *(Orenov)*;

Simon Oakland *(Belka)*; Barbara Hines *(Foreign Exchange Student)*; Marion Javits *(Miss Mellish)*; Michael Lane *(Glinka)*; Jack Benny *(Mr. Cosgrove)*; Kam Tong *(Lee Wong)*; Larri Thomas *(Dancing Girl)*.

Cinderfella
Paramount, 1960
91 minutes — Color
PRODUCER: Jerry Lewis. DIRECTOR: Frank Tashlin. SCREENPLAY: Frank Tashlin, *based on a story by* Jerry Lewis. MUSIC: Walter Scharf. EDITOR: Arthur P. Schmidt. MAKE-UP: Wally Westmore and Jack Stone. PHOTOGRAPHY: Haskell Boggs). SOUND: Bud Fehlman, Charles Grenzbach and Gene Merritt.

CAST: Jerry Lewis *(Cinderfella)*; Ed Wynn *(Fairy Godfather)*; Judith Anderson *(Wicked Stepmother)*; Henry Silva *(Maximillian)*; Robert Hutton *(Rupert)*; Count Basie *(Himself)*; Joe Williams *(Band Vocalist)*; Anna Maria Alberghetti *(Princess Charming)*; Barry Gordon *(Fella at age eleven)*; Del Moore *(Radio Announcer)*; Robert Jordan *(Reporter)*; Anne Dore *(Lady in Waiting)*; Francesca Bellini, Frances McHale, Darlene Tompkins, **Joi Lansing** *(scene deleted)*.

Marriage on the Rocks
Warner Bros., 1965
109 minutes — Color
PRODUCER: William H. Daniels. DIRECTOR: Jack Donohue. SCREENPLAY: Cy Howard, *based on the story* "Community Property" *by* Cy Howard. MUSIC: Nelson Riddle. EDITOR: Sam O'Steen. MAKE-UP: Gordon Bau. PHOTOGRAPHY: William H. Daniels. SOUND: Francis E. Stahl.

CAST: Frank Sinatra *(Dan Edwards)*; Deborah Kerr *(Valerie Edwards)*; Dean Martin *(Ernie Brewer)*; Cesar Romero *(Miguel Santos)*; Hermione Baddeley *(Jeannie MacPherson)*; Tony Bill *(Jim Blake)*; John McGiver *(Shad Nathan)*; Nancy Sinatra *(Tracy Edwards)*; Davey Davison *(Lisa Sterling)*; **Joi Lansing** *(Lola)*; Michel Petit *(David Edwards)*; Trini Lopez *(Himself)*; Tara Ashton *(Bunny)*; Sigrid Valdis *(Kitty)*; Kathleen Freeman *(Miss Blight)*; DeForest Kelley *(Mr. Turner)*; Flip Mark *(Rollo)*.

Hillbillys in a Haunted House
Woolner Bros., 1967
86 minutes — Color
PRODUCER: Bernard Woolner. **DIRECTOR**: Jean Yarbrough.
SCREENPLAY: Duke Yelton. **MUSIC**: Hal Borne. **EDITOR**: Holbrook Todd. **MAKE-UP**: Lew La Cava. **PHOTOGRAPHY**: Vaughn Wilkins. **SOUND**: Bob Post.

CAST: Ferlin Husky *(Woody Wetherby);* **Joi Lansing** *(Boots Malone);* Don Bowman *(Jeepers);* John Carradine *(Dr. Himmil);* Lon Chaney Jr. *(Maximillian);* Linda Ho *(Madame Wong);* Basil Rathbone *(Gregor);* Molly Bee, Merle Haggard, Sonny James, Jim Kent, Marcella Wright *(Themselves — Singers);* Richard Webb *(Jim Meadows);* Larry Barton, Pat Patterson, Marshall Wright *(Hillbillies);* George Barrows *(Anatole the Gorilla);* Allen Jung *(Dr. Fu);* Virginia Lee *(Ming Toy).*

Bigfoot
Ellman Film Enterprises, 1970
84 minutes — Color
PRODUCER: Anthony Cardoza, Bill Reardon and Herman Tomlin.
DIRECTOR: Robert F. Slatzer. **SCREENPLAY**: Robert F. Slatzer and James Gordon White. **MUSIC**: Richard A. Podolor. **EDITOR**: Hugo Grimaldi and Bud Hoffman. **MAKE-UP**: Louis Lane. **PHOTOGRAPHY**: William S. Hong. **SOUND**: Ken Carlson, Bob Dietz and James Fullerton.

CAST: John Carradine *(Jasper B. Hawks);* **Joi Lansing** *(Joi Landis);* John Mitchum *(Elmer Briggs);* Judith Jordan *(Chris);* Christopher Mitchum *(Rick);* James Craig *(Cyrus);* Joy Wilkerson *(Peggy);* Lindsay Crosby *(Wheels);* Ken Maynard *(Mr. Bennett);* Dorothy Keller *(Nellie Bennett);* Doodles Weaver *(Forest Ranger);* Noble 'Kid'Chissell *(Hardrock);* Del 'Sonny' West *(Mike);* Suzy Crosby *(Suzy);* Jennifer Bishop *(Bobbi);* Gloria Hill, Nancy Hunter *(Female Creature).*

When a Girl's Beautiful, 1947.

Linda Be Good, 1947.

Linda Be Good lobby card, 1947.

Easter Parade, with Joy standing behind Ann Miller, 1948.

Julia Misbehaves, with Greer Garson and Lola Albright, 1948.

The Girl From Jones Beach, 1949.

Lobby card for *Holiday Rhythm*, 1950.

FBI Girl, 1951.

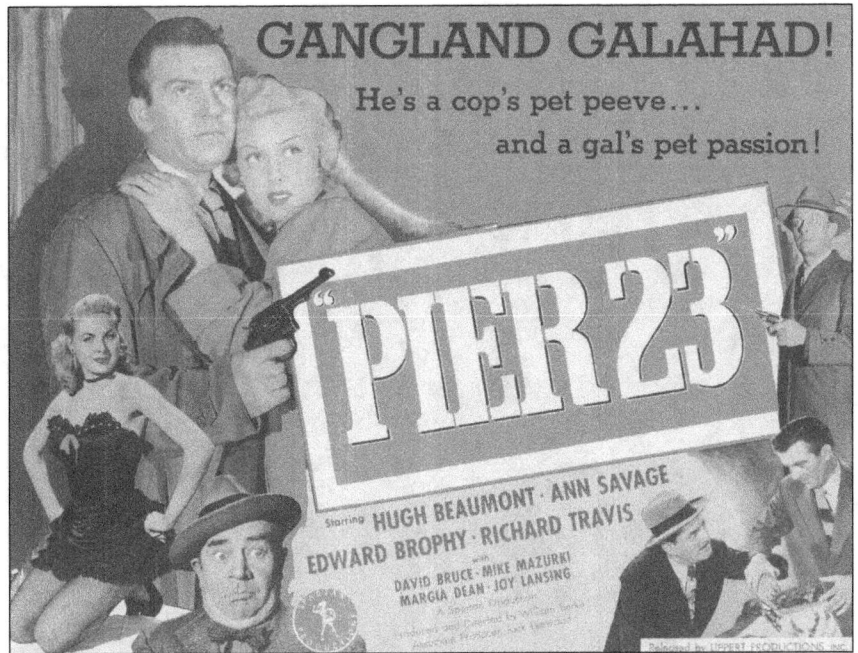

Pier 23 movie poster, 1951.

Pier 23, with Hugh Beaumont, 1951.

The French Line lobby card, 1953.

Son of Sinbad, with Vincent Price, Mari Blanchard, Bette Arlen and Doreen Woodbury, 1955.

So You Want to be a Policeman, 1955.

The Brave One, with Rodolfo Hoyos Jr. and Carlos Navarro, 1956.

Hot Cars, with John Bromfield, 1956.

Hot Cars, 1956.

Above and Below: *Hot Shots*, with Huntz Hall, 1956.

But Not for Me, with Clark Gable and Lee Cobb Jr., 1959.

The Atomic Submarine, with Arthur Franz, 1959.

Who Was That Lady, with Dean Martin, Barbara Nichols and Tony Curtis, 1960.

Marriage on the Rocks movie poster, 1965.

Marriage on the Rocks, with Dean Martin, 1965.

Hillbillys in a Haunted House, with Don Bowman and Ferlin Husky, 1967.

Hillbillys in a Haunted House, with Ferlin Husky and Don Bowman, 1967.

Bigfoot, 1969.

Publicity photo for *Klondike*, 1960.

Television Appearances

1949

Sadie and Sally: Hal Roach Studios. Joy Lansing *(Sadie)*.

1952

Gang Busters: NBC. "The Suma Case." Joy Lansing *(Cathy)*.

The Racket Squad: CBS — March 13. "Racket Squad." Joy Lansing *(Sandra)*.

1953

Your Jeweler's Showcase: CBS — December 22. "Farewell to Birdie McKeever."

1954

The Jack Carson Show: NBC. Joy Lansing *(Herself)*.

I Led 3 Lives: DUMONT TELEVISION NETWORK. "Deportation." Joy Lansing *(Salesgirl)*.

The Lone Wolf: "The Mexico Story — Aztec Treasure."

Meet Corliss Archer: CBS. "Harry and the Soap Opera Queen." Joy Lansing *(Louise, Soap Opera Queen)*.

Where's Raymond? The Ray Bolger Show. ABC — April 15. "The Enlisted Reserves." Joy Lansing *(Sergeant Martin's Girlfriend)*.

California. CBS — October 17. Joy Lansing *(Silent Movie Actress)*.

General Electric Theater: CBS — November 21. "The Face is Familiar." Joy Lansing *(Marie)*.

1955

The Bob Cummings Show: NBC — January 2. "Calling Doctor Baxter." Joy Lansing *(Bridal Model)*.

Adventures of Wild Bill Hickok: CBS — January 30. "To the Highest Bidder." Joy Lansing *(Dolores Carter)*.

So This is Hollywood: NBC — February 5. "He Done Her Wrong." Joy Lansing *(The Blonde)*.

December Bride: CBS — February 21. "Jealousy." Joy Lansing *(Miss Sullivan)*.

It's a Great Life: NBC — April 5. "The Hospital." Joy Lansing *(Miss Standish)*.

Schlitz Playhouse of Stars: CBS — April 22. "Who's the Blonde." *(The Blonde)*.

Who's the Blonde, with Alexander Campbell and Maxine Cooper, 1955.

Damon Runyon Theater: CBS — April 30. "All is Not Gold."

December Bride: CBS — October 24. "Ruth Neglects Matt." Joy Lansing *(Linda)*.

Four Star Playhouse: CBS — November 10. "The Devil to Pay." Joi Lansing *(Miss Wilson)*.

Four Star Playhouse: CBS — November 17. "Here Comes the Suit." Joi Lansing *(Elevator Operator)*.

The Ford Television Theatre: NBC — November 17. "A Smattering of Bliss." Joi Lansing *(Inez Hamilton)*.

Four Star Playhouse: CBS — November 25. "Marked Down." Joi Lansing *(Secretary)*.

The People's Choice: NBC — November 24. "Sock Hires Mandy." Joi Lansing *(Vicki Summers)*.

The Bob Cummings Show: NBC — December 29. "The Sheik." Joi Lansing *(Shirley Swanson)*.

1956

It's a Great Life: NBC — January 8. "Beauty Contest." Joi Lansing *(Betty Clark)*.

Cavalcade of America: ABC — January 17. "The Prison Within." Joi Lansing *(Florence)*.

Henry Fonda Presents the Star and the Story: January 21. "The Difficult Age." Joi Lansing *(Mitzi)*.

Cavalcade of America: ABC — January 24. "Star and Shield."

The Bob Cummings Show: NBC — January 26. "The Acid Test." Joi Lansing *(Shirley Swanson)*.

Celebrity Playhouse: NBC — January 31. "Bachelor Husband." Joi Lansing *(Eartha Svensen)*.

The Bob Cummings Show: CBS — February 9. "Too Many Women." Joi Lansing *(Shirley Swanson)*.

The Bob Cummings Show: CBS — February 16. "Snow Bound." Joi Lansing *(Shirley Swanson)*.

Jane Wyman Presents the Fireside Theatre: NBC — March 20. "Shoot the Moon." Joi Lansing *(Terry)*.

The Bob Cummings Show: CBS — July 5. "The Petticoat Derby." Joi Lansing *(Shirley Swanson)*.

Conflict: ABC — October 16. "The Magic Brew." Joi Lansing *(Greta Belle Short)*.

The Bob Cummings Show: CBS — October 18. "Bob Batches It." Joi Lansing *(Shirley Swanson)*.

I Love Lucy: CBS — November 25. "Desert Island." Joi Lansing *(Herself)*.

Noah's Ark: NBC — December 11. "A Girl's Best Friend." Joi Lansing *(Barbara Windso)*.

1957

The Gale Storm Show: CBS — January 5. "Girls! Girls! Girls!" Joi Lansing *(Kristin)*.

The Bob Cummings Show: CBS — January 24. "The Models Revolt." Joi Lansing *(Shirley Swanson)*.

The Bob Cummings Show: CBS — January 31. "Bob Saves Doctor Chuck." Joi Lansing *(Shirley Swanson)*.

December Bride: CBS — February 4. "Study Group." Joi Lansing *(Candy)*.

Make Room for Daddy: ABC — March 14. "The Model." Joi Lansing *(Blonde Model)*.

The Bob Cummings Show: CBS — March 21. "Bob Meets the Mortons." Joi Lansing *(Shirley Swanson)*.

The Adventures of Ozzie and Harriet: CBS — April 3. "The Hawaiian Party." Joi Lansing *(Blonde)*.

Playhouse 90: CBS — April 11. "If You Knew Elizabeth." Joi Lansing *(Miss Swanson)*.

The People's Choice: NBC — May 30. "The Sophisticates." Joi Lansing *(Linda Archer)*.

The Adventures of Ozzie and Harriet: CBS — June 5. "The Coffee Table" Joi Lansing *(Assistant Instructor in Woodworking Shop)*.

Climax! CBS — June 6. "Mr. Runyon of Broadway." Joi Lansing *(Lucy)*.

The Adventures of Ozzie and Harriet: CBS — October 30. "Mystery Shopper." Joi Lansing *(Blonde)*.

Perry Mason: CBS — November 9. "The Case of the Crimson Kiss." Joi Lansing *(Vera Payson)*.

Make Room for Daddy: ABC — December 2. "Terry, the Breadwinner." Joi Lansing *(Alysse)*.

The Bob Cummings Show: NBC — November 26. "Thanksgiving at Grandpa's." Joi Lansing *(Shirley Swanson)*.

The Bob Cummings Show: NBC — December 10. "Bob, the Gunslinger." Joi Lansing *(Shirley Swanson)*.

1958

The Bob Cummings Show: NBC — January 7. "Bob and Harvey Go Hunting." Joi Lansing *(Shirley Swanson)*.

The Bob Cummings Show: NBC — January 14. "Bob and Harvey Get Ambushed." Joi Lansing *(Shirley Swanson)*.

Sugarfoot. ABC — January 21. "Bullet Proof." Joi Lansing *(Peaches)*.

The Bob Cummings Show: NBC — February 4. "Bob falls for Schulzy." Joi Lansing *(Shirley Swanson)*.

The Frank Sinatra Show: ABC — February 28. Joi Lansing *(Herself)*.

State Trooper: NBC — March 1. "The Case of the Happy Dragon." Joi Lansing *(Angie)*.

Studio 57: DUMONT TELEVISION NETWORK. — March 11. "The Starmaker."

The Bob Cummings Show: NBC — March 11. "Bob Gets Harvey a Raise." Joi Lansing *(Shirley Swanson)*.

Mike Hammer: REVUE PRODUCTIONS — March 14. "Lead Ache." Joi Lansing *(Jackie LaRue)*.

The Bob Cummings Show: NBC — March 18. "Bob Saves Harvey." Joi Lansing *(Shirley Swanson)*.

The Bob Cummings Show: NBC — March 25. "Bob Goes Bird Watching." Joi Lansing *(Shirley Swanson).*

Adventures of Superman: SUPERMAN INC. — March 31. "Superman's Wife." Joi Lansing *(Sgt. Helen J. O'Hara).*

Maverick: ABC — April 13. "Seeds of Deception." Joi Lansing *(Doll Hayes).*

The Bob Cummings Show: NBC — May 13. "Grandpa's Old Buddy." Joi Lansing *(Shirley Swanson).*

The Thin Man: NBC — May 30. "Kappa Kappa Kaper." Joi Lansing *(Girl at Carriage).*

1959

The Bob Cummings Show: NBC — January 6. "Bob's Boyhood Love Image." Joi Lansing *(Shirley Swanson).*

Sea Hunt: MGM TV — February 1. "Monte Cristo." Joi Lansing *(Laura Pepper).*

The Jack Benny Program: CBS — February 8. "Jack Goes to a Nightclub." Joi Lansing *(Bessie Gifford).*

The Bob Cummings Show: NBC — February 17. "Bob, the Babysitter." Joi Lansing *(Shirley Swanson).*

Lux Playhouse: CBS — March 6. "Stand-In for Murder."

The Lucy-Desi Comedy Hour: CBS — April 13. "Lucy Wants a Career." Joi Lansing *(Miss Low Neck).*

Richard Diamond, Private Detective: CBS — May 10. "Jukebox." Joi Lansing *(Diane).*

The Bob Cummings Show: NBC — June 23. "Bob, the Last Bachelor." Joi Lansing *(Shirley Swanson).*

Markham: CBS — July 11. "Forty-Two on a Rope." Joi Lansing *(Hatcheck Girl).*

General Electric Theater: CBS — October 11. "Night Club." Joi Lansing *(Babysitter).*

Maverick, with James Garner, 1958.

Bat Masterson: NBC — October 22. "No Funeral for Thorne." Joi Lansing *(Sapphira Gardiner)*.

1960

This Man Dawson: ZIV — January 1. "Accessory to Murder." Joi Lansing *(Carol Dawn)*.

The Untouchables: ABC — January 14. "The Noise of Death." Joi Lansing *(Georgina Jones)*.

The Dennis O'Keefe Show: CBS — February 9. "Follow That Mink." Joi Lansing *(Mavis)*.

The Adventures of Ozzie and Harriet: ABC — February 17. "Uninvited Guests." Joi Lansing *(Blonde)*.

The Bob Hope Show: NBC — April 20. Joi Lansing *(Herself)*.

Mr. Lucky: CBS — June 18. "Election Bet." Joi Lansing *(Evelyn)*.

Klondike: NBC — October 10. "Klondike Fever." Joi Lansing *(Goldie)*.

Klondike: NBC — October 24. "River of Gold." Joi Lansing *(Goldie)*.

Klondike: NBC — October 31. "Saints and Stickups." Joi Lansing *(Goldie)*.

Klondike: NBC — November 21. "Swoger's Mule." Joi Lansing *(Goldie)*.

Klondike: NBC — December 5. "Taste of Danger." Joi Lansing *(Goldie)*.

Here's Hollywood: NBC — December 28. Joi Lansing *(Herself)*.

1961

Klondike: NBC — January 30. "The Man Who Owned Skagway." Joi Lansing *(Goldie)*.

Klondike: NBC — February 13. "The Hostages." Joi Lansing *(Goldie)*.

1962

The Bob Hope Show: NBC — February 27. Joi Lansing *(Herself)*.

1963

The Joey Bishop Show: NBC — January 1. "Joey Leaves Ellie." Joi Lansing *(Gloria Colby).*

The Adventures of Ozzie and Harriet: ABC — January 31. "Roadside Courtesy." Joi Lansing *(Clubwoman).*

The Beverly Hillbillies: CBS — February 6. "A Bride for Jed." Joi Lansing *(Gladys Flatt).*

Ben Jerrod: NBC — June.

The Joey Bishop Show, with Joey Bishop, 1963.

The Adventures of Ozzie and Harriet: ABC — September 18. "The Torn Dress." Joi Lansing *(Saleslady)*.

Rawhide: CBS — October 10. "Incident at El Grucero." Joi Lansing *(Dance Hall Girl)*.

1964

The Mike Douglas Show: CBS — January 31. Joi Lansing *(Herself)*.

The Beverly Hillbillies: CBS — March 18. "Jed Throws a Wingding." Joi Lansing *(Gladys Flatt)*.

1965

The Merv Griffin Show: June 8. Joi Lansing *(Herself)*.

1966

The Beverly Hillbillies: CBS — March 16. "Flatt and Scruggs Return." Joi Lansing *(Gladys Flatt)*.

The Beverly Hillbillies, with Max Baer, 1967.

1967

The Beverly Hillbillies: CBS — March 29. "Delovely and Scruggs." Joi Lansing *(Gladys Flatt).*

The Joey Bishop Show: ABC — June 6. Joi Lansing *(Herself).*

The Joey Bishop Show: ABC — June 29. Joi Lansing *(Herself).*

The Jones Boys: August 14.

1968

Petticoat Junction: CBS — January 13. "Steve, the Apple Polisher." Joi Lansing *(Millicent Marshall).*

The Mike Douglas Show: March 15. Joi Lansing *(Herself).*

The Steve Allen Show: KTLA — June 28. Joi Lansing *(Herself).*

The Mother's in Law: NBC — November 20. "Take Her, He's Mine." Joi Lansing *(Barbara).*

The Beverly Hillbillies: CBS — November 20. "Bonnie, Flatt and Scruggs." Joi Lansing *(Gladys Flatt).*

George Jessel's Here Come the Stars. December 6. "Don Rickles." Joi Lansing *(Herself).*

1969

The Dean Martin Show: NBC — April 10. Joi Lansing *(Herself).*

1970

The Governor and J.J.: NBC — December 16. "P.S. I Don't Love You." Joi Lansing *(Joan Brock).*

1971

The Virginia Graham Show: March 3, 1971. Joi Lansing *(Herself)*

Sadie and Sally, with Lois Hall, 1948.

The Face is Familiar, with Jack Benny and Jean Willes, 1954.

Where's Raymond, The Ray Bolger Show, 1954.

A Smattering of Bliss, 1955.

The Devil to Pay, with Charles Boyer, 1955.

The People's Choice, "Sock Hires Mandy," with Jackie Cooper, 1955.

Bachelor Husband, with Richard Denning and Phyllis Kirk, 1956.

It's a Great Life, with William Bishop, 1956.

Noah's Ark, with Paul Burke, 1956.

Shoot the Moon, with Ozzie Nelson, 1956.

Climax, with Jack Lord, 1957.

Make Room for Daddy, "The Model," with Danny Thomas, Barbara Logan and Elaine Edwards, 1957.

The Adventures of Ozzie and Harriet, "Mystery Shopper," with David Nelson, 1957.

The Bob Cummings Show, "The Models Revolt," with Margie Tenney and Carole Conn, 1957.

Mike Hammer, with Darren McGavin, 1958.

The Bob Cummings Show, "Bob Gets Harvey a Raise," with Bob Cummings and Lisa Gaye, 1958.

The Bob Cummings Show, with Bob Cummings and Lisa Gaye, 1958.

The Bob Cummings Show, 1958.

Bat Masterson, 1959.

Markham, with Ray Milland, 1959.

Night Club, with Glenda Farrell, 1959.

The Jack Benny Show, with Danny Thomas and Jack Benny, 1959.

Klondike, with James Coburn, 1960.

Klondike, 1960.

Klondike, with Ralph Taeger, 1960.

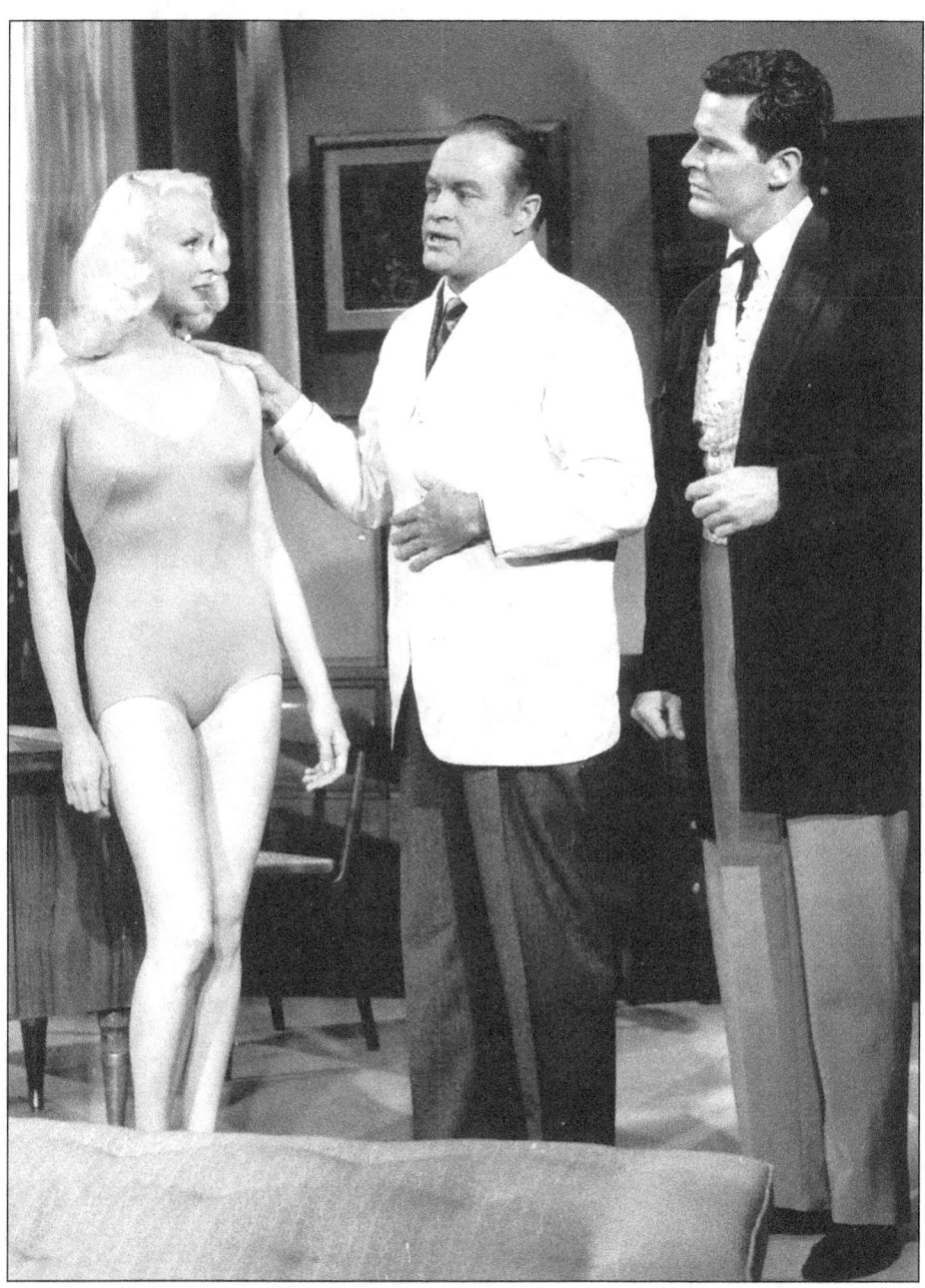

The Bob Hope Show, with Bob Hope and James Garner, 1960.

Ben Jerrod with Don Collier, 1963.

The Adventures of Ozzie and Harriet, "The Torn Dress," with Rick Nelson, 1963.

1947.

Pin-Ups

1949.

1951.

1954.

1955.

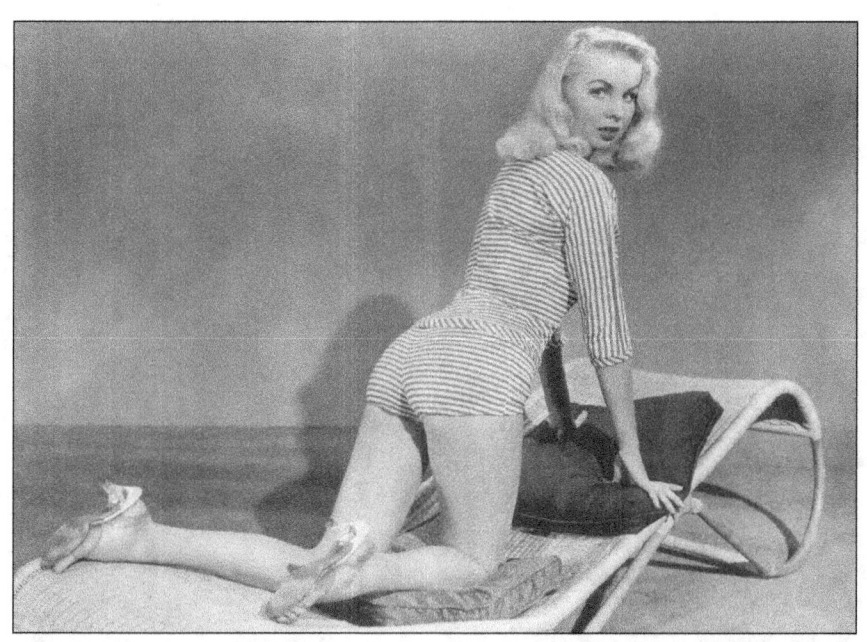

Publicity photos for *Hot Shots,* 1956.

1958.

1959.

1959.

Publicity photo for *Marriage on the Rocks*, 1965.

April, 1946 — USA.

Magazine Cover Gallery

March, 1948 — France.

October, 1948 — USA.

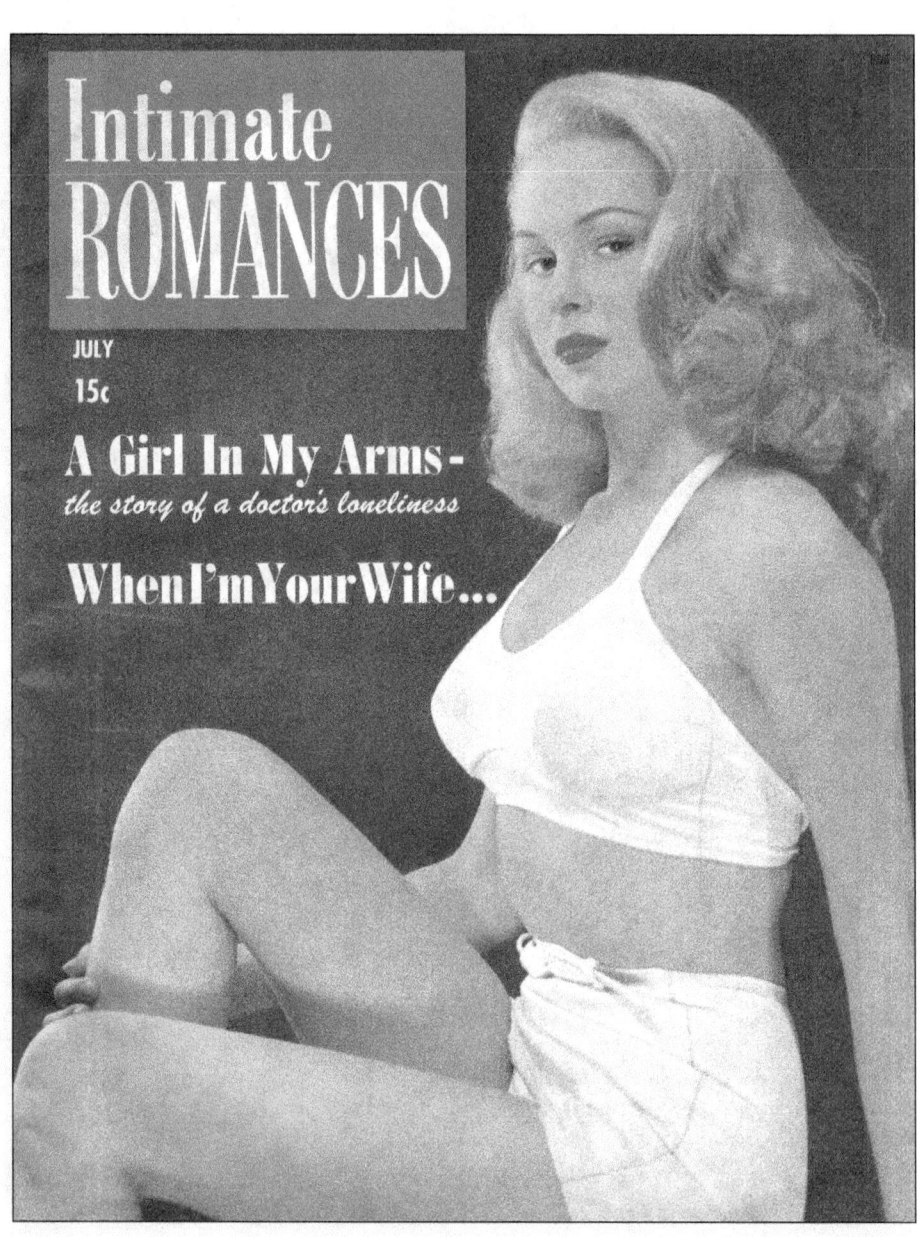

July, 1948 — USA.

March, 1949 — USA.

April, 1949 — USA.

April, 1949 — USA (International Edition).

May, 1949 — USA.

September, 1949 — USA.

November, 1949 — USA.

May, 1951 — USA.

August, 1952 — Italy.

February, 1954 — USA.

November, 1954 — USA.

March, 1955 — USA.

June, 1955 — USA.

August, 1955 — United Kingdom.

July, 1956 — Italy.

July, 1956 — USA.

October, 1956 — USA.

October, 1956 — USA.

June, 1957 — USA.

1959 — Brasil.

October, 1959 — USA.

August, 1965 — USA.

June, 1968 — USA.

December, 1969 — USA.

Bibliography

Albright, Brian. *Wild Beyond Belief! Interviews with Exploitation Filmmakers of the 1960s and 1970s.* Jefferson: McFarland & Company, Inc., Publishers, 2008.

Bernard, Susan. *Bernard of Hollywood — The Ultimate Pin-up book.* Cologne: Taschen, 2002.

Capra, Frank. *The Name Above the Title — An Autobiography.* New York: The MacMillan Company, 1971.

Dougherty, Joseph. *Comfort and Joi.* New York: iUniverse, Inc., 2005.

Eliot, Marc. *Reagan — The Hollywood Years.* New York: Random House LLC, 2008.

Fitzgerald, Michael G. and Magers, Boyd. *Ladies of the Western.* Jefferson: McFarland & Company, Inc., Publishers, 2010.

Fox, Col. Wesley L. *Marine Rifleman — Forty-Three Years in the Corps.* US: Potomac Book's, Inc., 2002.

Henning, Ruth. *The First Beverly Hillbilly — The Untold Story of the Creator of Rural TV Comedy.* Kansas City: Woodneath Press, 2017.

Hunter, Alexis. *Joi Lansing — A Body to Die For. A Love Story.* Albany: Bear Manor Media, 2015.

Kleno, Larry. *Kim Novak on Camera.* New York: A.S. Barnes & Company, Inc., 1980.

Koper, Richard. *That Kind of Woman — The Life and Career of Barbara Nichols.* Albany: Bear Manor Media, 2016.

Lertzman, Richard A. & Birnes, William J., *Dr. Feelgood.* New York: Skyhorse Publishing, 2013.

Marx, Bill. *Son of Harpo Speaks.* Duncan: Bear Manor Media, 2010.

Smith, Don G. *Lon Chaney, Jr.: Horror Film Star, 1906-1973.* Jefferson: McFarland & Company, Inc., Publishers, 1996.

Van Doren, Mamie and Aveilhe, Art. *Playing the Field — Sex, Stardom, Love, and Life in Hollywood.* Newport Beach, CA: Starlet Suave Books, 2013.

Weaver, Tom. *Eye on Science Fiction.* Jefferson: McFarland & Company, Inc., Publishers, 2003.

Index

Albright, Lola 50, 54, 213, 214, 216, *237*
Alphin, Pat *44*, 212
Angelich, Lauren 181
Anthony, Ray 115, *124*, 156, 224
Arden, Eve 18
Arlen, Bette 215, 216, 221, 223, *240*
Arnaz, Desi 94, 95, 137, 230
Astaire, Fred 49, 75, 76, 153, 213, 215, 224, *225*

Baer Jr, Max 147, *260*
Ball, Lucille 94, 95, 118
Ballard, Kaye 18
Beaumont, Hugh 64, 212, 218, *239*
Bennett, Pete *203*
Benny, Jack 76, 115, *128*, 233, 256, *262*, *288*
Bishop, Joey 184, *259*
Bishop, William *268*
Blanchard, Mari 136, 137, 218, 223, *240*
Bolger, Ray *263*
Bowman, Don 234, *247*, *248*
Boyer, Charles 78, 79, *265*
Bracken, Eddie 169, 216, 219
Bromfield, John *93*, 228, *242*
Brown, Jack Glen 31, 53, 134
Burke, Paul *269*
Burns, Lilian 48
Buttons, Red 168, 172

Caesar, Sid 183, *189*
Campbell, Alexander *252*
Capra, Frank 106, *112*, 230
Cardiff, Jack 77, 98, 227
Caron, Leslie 76, 165, 220, 224
Carradine, John 170, 183, 224, 234, *248*
Champlin, Charles 171
Chance, Larry 67
Chaney Jr, Lon 170, 212, 234.
Chase, Barrie 66, 75, 220, 224
Clements, Stanley 99, 100, 228

Cobb Jr, Lee 230, *241*
Coburn, James 136, 137, *282*
Collier, Don *286*
Conn, Carole *274*
Connolly, Mike 108, 122
Coogan, Jackie 192-194, *202*
Cooper, Jackie *266*
Cooper, Maxine *252*
Corcoran, Bill 14, 34, 109, 196
Corman, Roger 196
Crayne, Dani 104
Cumming, Robert 77, 89, *90*, 91, 103, 116, 173, *276*, *277*
Czar, Nancy 182

Davis, Lisa 106, 230
Davis Jr., Sammy 21, 108, 119
Dean, Margia 65, 218
Denning, Richard *267*
De Carvalho, Michel *see* Ray, Michel
De Salvo, Ron 192, 193, *194*, 195, 207
Dolive, Bill 200, *205*
Dors, Diana 93, 96, 171
Edwards, Elaine *272*

English, Marla 67, 223
Ekberg, Anita 44
Evans, Ray 25, 150, 154, 156, 164

Farrell, Glenda 29, 280
Foster, Bob 78, 96, 98
Fox, Wesley L. 96, *97*
Franz, Arthur 117, 232, *245*
Frazee, Jane 76, *86*, *222*, 226, 227
Fuller, Lance 62, *63*, 64, 66, 67, 220

Gable, Clark 47, 54, 116, *125*, 217, 231, *244*
Gabor, Zsa Zsa 61, 106, 195, 229, 230
Garland, Judy 49, 50, 155, 165, 213, 216

329

Garner, James *257*, *285*
Garrett, Betty 79, 214
Garson, Greer 213, *237*
Gaye, Lisa *276*, *277*
Giles, Sandra 115, 116, 156, 166
Grable, Betty 73
Graham, Sheilah 73, 119
Griffin, Stephanie 74, 223

Haas, Hugo 115
Hall, Huntz 99, 100, 228, *243*
Hall, Lois 51, *262*
Halsey, Brett 63, 117, 232
Hargitay, Mickey 115, 185, 186
Hayes, Bill 192, 194
Henning, Paul 89, 90, 116, 147, 168
Hickman, Dwayne 89,
Hitchcock, Alfred 74, 95, 223
Hodges, Eddie 16, 107, 231
Hope, Bob *285*
Hoyos Jr, Rodolfo 77, *86*, 228, *241*
Huff, Dorothy *44*, 211, 212
Hughes, Howard 67, 74, 219, 221, 223
Hunter, Alexis aka Rachel 7, 14, 18, 34, 73, 109, 149, 156, 174, 184-187, 197-200, *204*, 207, 209, 234
Husky, Ferlin 170, 234, *247*, *248*
Hutchins, Will 16, 103, 105
Hyde, Johnny 54

Jason, Rick 94, 95, 105, 230
Jergens, Adele 39, 40, *44*, *45*, 61, 211
Johnson, Van 104, 105, *111*, 216
Jordan, Joanne 74, 219, 223
Jordan Judith 183, *189*, 234

Kayne, Jan 65, 218, 220, *238*
Keith, Richard 95, 96
Kelly, Gene 63, 65, 214, 220
Kelly, Jack 105
Killgallen, Dorothy 24
Kirk, Phyllis *267*

Lawford, Peter 21, *53*, 213
Lee, Harriet 91
Lee, Ruta 115
Leigh, Janet 48, 120, 121, *219*, 229, 232
Lester, Buddy 168
Linn, Roberta 109

Lippert, Bob 170
Logan, Barbara *272*
Lopez, Trini 156, 164, 181, 186, 233
Lord, Jack *271*
Lorig, Gary 172
Loveland, Larry 33, 38, 39, 80, *91*, *104*, 152, 196, 207
Loveland, Vernon 32
Lupton, John 77
Luxemburg, Lenny 172-174

Machen, Eddie *177*
Mailer, Norman 25, 26
Mansfield, Jayne 93, 115, 116, *127*, 147, 153, 154, 165, 168, 169, 171, 181, 185, 191
Marin, Craig 198, *203*
Martin, Dean 21, 105, 109, 119, 120, *127*, 154, 163, 165, 169, 170, *177*, 183, 185, *189*, 195, 232, 233, *245*, *247*, 261
Martin, Tony 219
Marx, Bill 23, 134, 182
Marx, Mike 166, *167*, 168
Maxwell, Marilyn 61, 217
Mayer, Ken 25, 156, 208
Mayo, Virginia 501, 51, 73, 216
McGavin, Darren *275*
Meyer, Russ 196
Michaels, Dolores 74, 221, 223
Milland, Ray *279*
Miller, Ann 213, 219, *236*
Mitchell, Laurie 106, 230
Mitchum, Christopher 183, 184, 234
Monroe, Marilyn 17, 18, 24, 40, 49, 50, 54, 61, 73, 76, 78, 79, 96, 116, 168, 191, 207
Moore, Cleo 67, 73, 96, 115
Moore, Terry 76, 224
Morris, Carol 91, 115
Mumby, Diana 66, 223

Navarro, Carlos 77, *86*, 228, *241*
Nelson, David *273*
Nelson, Ozzie 91, *270*
Nelson, Rick 105, *287*
Newman, Paul 78
Nichols, Barbara 18, 106, 116, 119, 120, *127*, *129*, 232, *245*
Novak, Kim 24, 74, 93, 221, 223

O'Hanlon, George 76, *86*, 212, *222*, 226, 227, *241*

Pall, Gloria 16, 63, 74, 149, 221, 223, 229
Parks, Larry 79
Parsons, Louella 40, 50, 98
Piller, Sandra 166
Powell, Janey Lorraine *104*, 196
Presley, Elvis 116, 195
Price, Vincent 223, *240*

Quinn, Tandra 48

Raft, George 172
Ray, Michel 77, 228
Reagan, Ronald 50, 133, 216
Riordan, Christopher 16, 163
Roach, Hal 47, 51, 52, 251
Rodriguez, Santiago 23
Rooney, Mickey 50, 150
Russell, Jane 24, 74, 221

Sabrina 171
Safron, Jerome 61, 62
Selden, Stan 192, 193
Seymour, Maurice 198
Shane, Sara 48, 49, *57*, 74, *213*, 214, 215, 224
Sharpe, Karen 22
Shelton, Jack 38, 39, 48
Shupe, John 14, 18, 34, 37, 49, 80, 105, 152, 208
Shupe, Ray 'Grampy' 31, 34, *39*, 61, *62*, 63, *104*, 134, 146, 152
Shupe, Virginia Grace 31, *32*, 33, *36*, 37, 38, 52, 53, 61, *78*, *148*, 152, 200
Shupe-Rice, Annette Grace 31, 34, 61, *62*, 115
Slatzer, Bon 184, 207, 234
Sterling, Elaine *see* Shane, Sara
Sinatra, Frank 16, 18, 21, 103, 104, 107-109, *111*, *112*, 116, 118, 151, 152, 154, 163-166, 169, 172, *176*, 183, 207, 214, 230, 231, 233, 255

Smith, Edward 173
Stevens, Stella 155, 169

Taegar, Ralph 136, 137, *284*
Tenney, Margie *274*
Thibodeaux, Keith *see* Keith, Richard
Thomas, Danny *272*, *281*
Tobin, Dan 94, 95, 105, 230
Todd, Leslie 16, 23, 122, 199
Totter, Audrey 65, 218, *238*
Turner, Lana 24, 47, 48, 66, 73, 221

Van Doren, Mamie 16, 24, 66, 73, 93, 137, 147, 168, 171, 191, 219
Van Vooren, Monique 24
Vinton, Bobby *203*

Wasmansdorff, Carlton 80, 209
Watkins, Beverly 13, 49
Wayne, John 97, 98
Weld, Tuesday 109, 137
Welles, Orson 94, 95, 100, 105, 229, 230
White, James Gordon 184. 234
Wilkinson, June 199, 200
Willes, Jean 76, *262*
Williams, Esther 48, 214, 215
Wilson, Earl 14, 108
Wolfberg, Lee 181
Woodbury, Doreen 212, 223, *240*
Wynn, Keenan 106-108, *111*, 215, 229, 231

York, Francine 17

Joi Lansing as featured with other Hollywood blondes in a cartoon tribute by Stephen B. Whatley.

About The Author

RICHARD KOPER (1970), started collecting film memorabilia at the age of thirteen, after seeing *Some Like it Hot* (1959) with Marilyn Monroe. Through Marilyn, he found out about the other sexy flaxen-haired actresses of the 1950s.

Richard holds an impressive collection of vintage photos, magazines, movie posters and other film memorabilia. So far, he has written four books about his favorite subject, the blonde bombshell, and hopes to see many more published by BearManor Media in the years to come.

Apart from collecting, researching and writing, Richard holds a day job as a MDFT-family therapist.

Bear Manor Media

Classic Cinema.
Timeless TV.
Retro Radio.

WWW.BEARMANORMEDIA.COM

www.ingramcontent.com/pod-product-compliance
Lightning Source LLC
Chambersburg PA
CBHW071955220426
43662CB00009B/1140